Best Easy Day Hikes
Nashville

Help Us Keep This Guide Up to Date

Every effort has been made by the author and editors to make this guide as accurate and useful as possible. However, many things can change after a guide is published—trails are rerouted, regulations change, facilities come under new management, etc.

We would appreciate hearing from you concerning your experiences with this guide and how you feel it could be improved and kept up to date. While we may not be able to respond to all comments and suggestions, we'll take them to heart and we'll also make certain to share them with the author. Please send your comments and suggestions to the following address:

GPP
Reader Response/Editorial Department
P.O. Box 480
Guilford, CT 06437

Or you may e-mail us at:

editorial@GlobePequot.com

Thanks for your input, and happy trails!

Best Easy Day Hikes Series

Best Easy Day Hikes
Nashville

Keith Stelter

FALCONGUIDES

GUILFORD, CONNECTICUT
HELENA, MONTANA
AN IMPRINT OF GLOBE PEQUOT PRESS

FALCONGUIDES®

FalconGuides is an imprint of Globe Pequot Press.

Falcon, FalconGuides, and Outfit Your Mind are registered trademarks of Morris Book Publishing, LLC.

TOPO! Explorer software and SuperQuad source maps courtesy of National Geographic Maps. For information about TOPO! Explorer, TOPO!, and Nat Geo Maps products, go to www.topo.com or www .natgeomaps.com.

Maps created by Mapping Specialists Inc. © Morris Book Publishing, LLC.

Project editor: David Legere

Library of Congress Cataloging-in-Publication Data is available on file.

ISBN 978-0-7627-5981-1

Printed in the United States of America

10 9 8 7 6 5 4 3 2 1

Contents

Overview Map

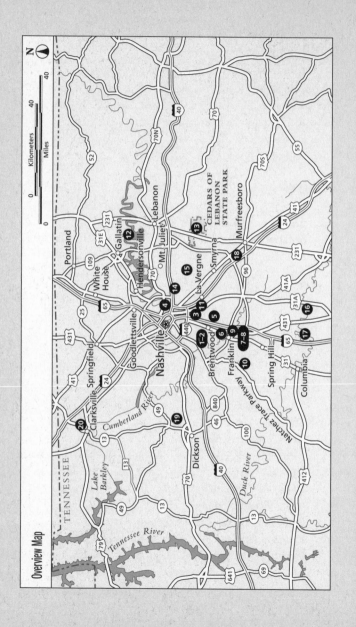

Acknowledgments

Many people helped make this book possible, and a few went "beyond the call of duty." Thanks to Mark, Scott, and Kay Stelter for their encouragement, ideas, patience, and proofreading; Nate Enloe for his general help; and Kevin Stelter, Olivia and Justin Stelter, and Shae Simpkins with Madison for hiking and journaling with me. Special thanks to Kay and Rod Heller for their Southern hospitality in allowing me to use their guesthouse as my base while in Nashville. Thanks also to Thurman Mullins, park superintendent at Long Hunter State Park. Dozens of other people provided information about the history, geology, flora, fauna, and karst areas and hikes they considered "the best easy day hikes near Nashville." I appreciate their work and thank all of them.

Introduction

The purpose of this guide is to introduce readers to the variety of hiking opportunities in the Nashville area. In many hiking guides the hike descriptions are generally point-to-point narratives, getting you safely from the trailhead to the trail's end and back again. However, including information on area flora, fauna, history, and geology adds a great deal of interest to many hikers, including families with young children.

Determining the best easy day hikes near Nashville was a combination of personal judgment about what level of hiker the hike was geared for and information from park staff and other hikers. Four of my favorite hikes are the varied trails at Long Hunter State Park, the interconnecting loops in Cedars of Lebanon State Park, the Greenways of Murfreesboro, and Henry Horton State Park trails. Hiking city and county trails offers a different experience from hiking in state parks and on backcountry trails. Most of the city trails are multipurpose and paved; a few are lighted at night, creating an entirely new hiking experience. Hiking these trails can also offer a distraction from the city itself, with its busy streets, buildings, and commerce. Surprisingly, many of the trails are in wooded areas, providing an unexpected degree of solitude.

The Nashville Parks and Recreation Department's trail system spans more than 60 miles. Enjoy the experience of hiking in middle Tennessee. The great ecological diversity of the territory, along with the flora, fauna, and karst geology, allows you to fashion trips that are much more than just "hikes in the woods." Some of the city hikes (trails) take place on sidewalks, some of which have been widened from the conventional 4 feet to as much as 13 feet. This allows many different people to use them—and some have been designed as "traffic lanes" (still called "trails") to accommodate commuters walking and biking to work as well as recreational hikers.

The Nature of Nashville

Hiking around Nashville is more than walking along rivers. Trails can be found in woods, forests, nature sanctuaries, downtown, or along an Army Corps of Engineers lake. Some are busy with hikers, joggers, and cyclists; others are secluded and far from downtown.

Weather

The Nashville climate is humid, with hot summers and cool winters. The area can experience snowfall, but the white stuff is usually gone the next morning. March signals the start of spring, with warmer weather and colorful displays of flowering trees and shrubs. From March until mid-May, temperatures average between 45 and 70 degrees. Summer brings warmer weather accompanied by high humidity. The relative humidity in Nashville is 83% in the morning and 60% in the afternoon. Mid- to late October has cooler temperatures that encourage brilliant fall colors. The average low temperature (37 degrees) occurs in January, and the average high (80 degrees) in July. The average yearly rainfall is 48.1 inches. The wettest month is May, averaging 5 inches. The driest month is October, with 2.87 inches of rain. Except for high temperatures in July and August and possible showers in May, the weather for hiking in Nashville is great.

Critters

You'll encounter mostly benign, sweet creatures on these trails, including deer, squirrels, rabbits, wild turkeys, and a variety of songbirds and shorebirds. More rarely seen (during daylight hours especially) are coyotes, raccoons, and opossums. Deer in some of the parks are remarkably tame and may linger on or close to the trail as you approach.

Nashville's parklands also are habitat for copperheads, water moccasins, and rattlesnakes, all venomous snakes. Encounters are infrequent, but you should be prepared to react properly if you run across a dangerous snake. Snakes generally only strike if they are threatened. You are too big to be dinner, so they typically avoid contact with humans. Keep your distance and they will keep theirs.

Safety and Preparation

Hiking in the Nashville area is generally safe. Still, hikers should be prepared, whether out for a short stroll along the Cumberland River waterfront or venturing into the forested Natchez Trace trails. Here is some specific advice:

Know the basics of first aid, including how to treat bleeding, bites and stings, and fractures, strains, and sprains. Pack a first-aid kit each time you head out for an excursion.

Familiarize yourself with the symptoms of heat exhaustion and heatstroke. Heat exhaustion symptoms include heavy sweating, muscle cramps, headache, dizziness, and fainting. Should you or anyone in your hiking party exhibit any of these symptoms, cool the person down immediately by rehydrating and getting him or her to an air-conditioned location. Cold showers also help reduce body temperature. Heatstroke is much more serious: The person may lose consciousness, and the skin is hot and dry to the touch. Call 911 immediately.

Regardless of the weather, the body needs a lot of water while hiking. A full thirty-two-ounce bottle is the minimum for these short hikes, but more is always better. Bring a full water bottle, whether water is available along the trail or not.

Don't drink from streams, rivers, creeks, or lakes without treating or filtering the water first. Waterways and bodies of water may host a variety of contaminants, including giardia, which can cause serious intestinal unrest.

Prepare for extremes of both heat and cold by dressing in layers.

Carry a backpack stocked with extra clothing, ample drinking water and food, and whatever goodies—like guidebooks, cameras, and binoculars—you might want.

Some area trails have cell phone coverage. Bring your device, but make sure you turn it off or set it on vibrate or silent while hiking. There is nothing like a "wake the dead"–loud ring to startle every creature, including fellow hikers.

Keep children under careful watch. The bigger rivers have dangerous currents and are not safe for swimming. Hazards along some of the trails include poison oak, uneven footing, and steep drop-offs. Make sure children don't stray from the designated route. Children should carry a plastic whistle; instruct them that if they become lost, they should stay in one place and blow the whistle to summon help.

Be prepared. Bring or wear clothes to protect you from cold, heat, or rain. Use maps to navigate (and do not rely solely on the maps included in this book).

Leave No Trace

Trails in the Nashville area and neighboring foothills are heavily used year-round. We, as trail users and advocates, must be especially vigilant to make sure our passage leaves no lasting mark. Here are some basic guidelines for preserving trails in the region:

Remain on the established route to avoid damaging trailside soils and plants. This is also a good rule of thumb to avoid trailside irritants like poison ivy.

Pack out all your trash, including biodegradable items like orange peels, and pack out garbage left by less considerate hikers too. Use portable toilets at trailheads or along the trail and keep water sources clean.

Don't pick wildflowers or gather rocks, antlers, feathers, or other treasures along the trail. Removing these items takes away from the next hiker's experience.

Be careful with fire. Use a camp stove for cooking. Be sure it's OK to build a campfire in the area you're visiting. Use an existing fire ring and keep your fire small. Use sticks from the ground as kindling. Burn all the wood to ash, and be sure the fire is completely out and cold before leaving.

Don't approach or feed wild creatures—the ground squirrel eyeing your snack food is best able to survive if it remains self-reliant. Control pets at all times.

Be kind to other visitors. Be courteous by not making loud noises while hiking, and be aware that you share the trail with others. Yield to other trail users when appropriate.

For more information about Leave No Trace, visit www.lnt.org.

How to Use This Guide

Twenty hikes are detailed in this guide, which is designed to be simple and easy to use. The overview map at the beginning of this book shows the location of each hike by hike number, keyed to the table of contents. Each hike includes a route map that shows all accessible roads and trails, points of interest, access to water, towns, landmarks, and geographical features. It also distinguishes trails from roads and paved roads from unpaved roads. The selected route is highlighted, and directional arrows point the way. It indicates the general outline of the hike, but due to scale restrictions, it is not as detailed as a park map might be or even as our "Miles and Directions" are. While most of the hikes are on clearly designated paths, use these route maps in conjunction with other resources.

To help you choose the right hike for you and your party, each hike description begins with a short summary of the adventure to follow. You'll learn about the trail terrain and what surprises the route has to offer. Next you'll find the quick, nitty-gritty details of the hike: hike distance and type (loop, lollipop, or out-and-back); approximate hiking time; difficulty rating; type of trail surface; best season for the hike; other trail users; canine compatibility; fees and permits; park schedule; and map resources, trail contacts, and additional information that will help you on your trek.

"Finding the trailhead" provides directions from Nashville right to where you'll want to park your car. **"The Hike"** is the meat of each chapter. Detailed and honest, it's a carefully researched impression of the trail. While it's impossible to cover everything, you can rest assured that you won't miss what's important. **"Miles and Directions"** provides mileage cues that identify all turns and trail name changes, as well as points of interest.

Don't feel restricted to the routes and trails mapped in this guide. Stick to marked trails, but be adventurous and use the book as a platform to discover new routes for yourself. One of the simplest ways to begin is to turn the map upside down and hike the trail in reverse. The change in perspective can make the hike feel quite different; it's like getting two hikes for one. You may wish to copy the directions for the course onto a small sheet of paper to help you as you hike, or you can photocopy the map. Otherwise, just slip the whole book in your pocket and take it with you.

Enjoy your time in the outdoors—and remember to pack out what you pack in.

Hike Selection

This guide describes trails that are accessible to every hiker, whether a visitor from out of town or someone lucky enough to live in Nashville. The hikes are no longer than 5 miles round-trip, and some are considerably shorter. They range in difficulty from flat excursions perfect for a family outing to more challenging treks in the rolling hills on Tennessee's Central Basin. While these trails are among the best, keep in mind that nearby trails, often in the same park or preserve, may offer options better suited to your needs. I've sought to space hikes throughout the Nashville area, so wherever your starting point, you'll find a great easy day hike nearby.

Difficulty Ratings

These are all easy hikes, but *easy* is a relative term. Some would argue that no hike involving any kind of climbing is easy, but in the Nashville area, rolling hills are a fact of life. To aid in the selection of a hike that suits a hiker's particular needs and abilities, each is rated *easy, moderate,* or *more challenging.* Bear in mind that even the most challenging routes can be made easy by hiking within your limits and taking rests when you need them.

- **Easy** hikes are generally short and flat, taking no longer than an hour to complete.

- **Moderate** hikes involve increased distance and relatively mild changes in elevation and will take one to two hours to complete.

- **More challenging** hikes feature some steep stretches, greater distances, and generally take longer than two hours to complete.

These are completely subjective ratings—consider that what you think is easy is entirely dependent on your level of fitness and the adequacy of your gear (primarily shoes). If you are hiking with a group, you should select a hike with a rating that's appropriate for the least fit and prepared in your party.

Approximate hiking times are based on the assumption that on flat ground, most walkers average 2 miles per hour. Adjust that rate by the steepness of the terrain and your level of fitness (subtract time if you're an aerobic animal and add time if you're hiking with kids), and you have a ballpark hiking duration. Be sure to add more time if you plan to picnic or take part in other activities like birding or photography.

Trail Finder

Best Hikes for Families

1   Edwin Warner Park: Cane Connector Trail
2   Radnor Lake State Natural Area: Spillway Trail
    and Lake Trail
3   Ellington Agricultural Center: Eagle Trail and
    Roberts Walk
5   Brentwood Greenway: River Park Trail
8   Pinkerton Park: Fort Granger Trail
11 Mill Creek Greenway Trail
13 Cedars of Lebanon State Park: Cedar Glade
    Interpretive Trail
14 Percy Priest Lake: Three Hickories Trail
15 Long Hunter State Park: Couchville Lake Trail
16 Henry Horton State Park: Wild Turkey Trail
18 Murfreesboro Greenway: College Street Pond
    Loop

Best Hikes for Lake, River, and Creek Lovers

2   Radnor Lake State Natural Area: Spillway Trail
    and Lake Trail
3   Ellington Agricultural Center: Eagle Trail and
    Roberts Walk
4   Nashville Greenway: Shelby Bottoms Nature Trail
5   Brentwood Greenway: River Park Trail
6   Brentwood: Deerwood Arboretum Trail
10 Natchez Trace: Garrison Creek Trail and
    Overlook Trail
11 Mill Creek Greenway Trail
12 Bledsoe Creek State Park: Loop and Shoreline
    Trails

Best Hikes for Nature Lovers and Birders

Best Hikes for Dogs

Map Legend

65	Interstate Highway
412	U.S. Highway
55	State Highway
	Local Road
- - - - - - -	Unpaved Road
▬▬▬▬▬	Featured Trail
- - - - - - - -	Trail
⌇	River/Creek
⌐ ⌐ ⌐	Local/State Park
	Marsh/Swamp
⬭	Body of Water
▭	Bench
▥▥▥▥▥	Boardwalk
⤙	Boat Launch
⏝	Bridge
▲	Campground
∧	Cave
•—•	Gate
🅿	Parking
🛱	Picnic Area
■	Point of Interest/Structure
🛉	Ranger Station
🚻	Restroom
○	Town
⑪	Trailhead
🔭	Viewpoint/Overlook
❓	Visitor/Information Center
🚰	Water

1 Edwin Warner Park: Cane Connector Trail

The trail combines portions of Edwin Warner and Percy Warner Parks. Views from the five bridges that cross Vaughn's Creek provide good photo ops. Portions of the trail follow sections of the Natchez Trace, which went from Nashville to Natchez, Mississippi.

Start: Cane Connector Trail trailhead, at the kiosk behind the Warner Park Nature Center
Distance: 2.0-mile out-and-back
Approximate hiking time: 1.5 hours
Difficulty: Easy
Trail surface: Dirt, rock
Best season: Year-round
Other trail users: Dog walkers
Canine compatibility: Leashed dogs permitted
Fees and permits: None required

Schedule: Dawn to dusk
Maps: USGS: Bellevue; trail maps and brochures available at the Warner Park Nature Center
Trail contact: Warner Park Nature Center, 7311 Highway 100, Nashville 37221; (615) 352-6299; www.nashville.gov /parks/wpnc
Other: Restrooms and water available at the Warner Park Nature Center. There is no potable water or restrooms on the trail.

Finding the trailhead: From the south side of Nashville, take I-40 West toward Memphis and go 9.2 miles. Take TN 251, exit 99, and turn left onto Old Hickory Boulevard/TN 251. Continue to follow Old Hickory Boulevard for 3.8 miles. Turn left onto TN 100 and follow it 0.6 mile to 7311 (TN 100). Turn into Edwin Warner Park and proceed to the nature center. *DeLorme Tennessee Atlas & Gazetteer:* Page 53 C5. GPS: N36 03.653 / W86 54.321

The Hike

The out-and-back Cane Connector Trail is truly a connector trail. It connects to the 4.5-mile Mossy Ridge Loop and the 2.0-mile Warner Woods Trail, thereby connecting the entire Warner Park Trail system. The trail is flat and 7 feet wide and has good tree cover.

Start the hike at the kiosk at the rear of the nature center in Edwin Warner Park. Head south, crossing the bridge over Vaughn's Creek. The creek may be dry, depending on the amount of rainfall and season of the year.

Follow the trail and cross a bridge on the left. Notice the variety of hardwood trees, including oak, beech, and maples. Cross Old Hickory Boulevard. Use caution, as this is a very busy highway with cars traveling at 45 miles per hour. Almost immediately go up five steps and cross another bridge. In the fall leaves will cover the trail; watch for tree roots on the trail. Bear slightly left and cross another bridge.

Pass a building about 300 feet on the left, which houses the Bob Brown Field Station. Continue until you reach a T. The left branch leads to the field station. Take the right branch, making a hard right, and take five steps up to cross another bridge. Take a hard left at the end of the bridge. The creek is now on the left but is not visible. Watch for butterflies, especially in the spring and fall. They tend to congregate around small pools of water. The trail flattens and heads slightly down. The creek and woods furnish ideal habitat for a variety of birds and animals, including deer. Look for deer and raccoon tracks.

Reach an asphalt park road and cross it to pick up the trail marked by a candy–striped post. In the fall, look for acorns and hickory nuts on the trail. They are a little difficult to open, but they are tasty and good to eat; take a few home and try them. In the spring and fall, spider webs may cross the trail.

Continue north, following the candy–striped blazes. The trail slopes slightly up. Look for several large shagbark hickory trees. Reach the T, which is the end of the trail. Here the Cane Connector Trail links up to Mossy Ridge Loop and the Warner Woods Trail. Folks that still have a lot of energy may want to take one of these. If not, backtrack to the trailhead.

Miles and Directions

0.0 Start at the Cane Connector Trail trailhead, at the kiosk at the rear of the nature center in Edwin Warner Park. The trail is identified with red-and-white-striped blazes.

0.1 Within 200 feet cross the bridge over Vaughn's Creek and make a hard right into the woods. Follow the trail as it crosses Old Hickory Boulevard into Percy Warner Park. Use caution!

0.15 Continue following the trail in a northeast direction. Make a hard right immediately before crossing another bridge over Vaughn's Creek. At the end of the bridge, make a hard left.

0.3 Bear left and go a short distance to another bridge. A building that houses the Bob Brown Field Station can be seen about 300 feet away on the left.

0.4 Make a hard right, heading east. There is an opening to the creek on the right. Take the short out-and-back to explore the creek. Return to the trail as it bears slightly left. Reach a T; take the right branch, and immediately make a hard right and cross another bridge.

0.6 Pass a candy-striped trail marker and reach an asphalt park road. Use caution and cross the road to the trail on the opposite side. Head north, going into the woods.

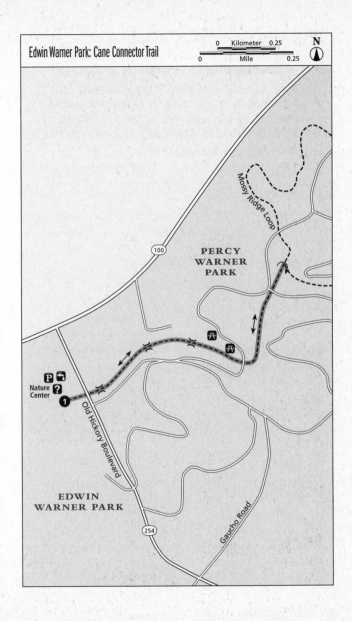

Edwin Warner Park: Cane Connector Trail

N

0 Kilometer 0.25
0 Mile 0.25

PERCY
WARNER
PARK

Mossy Ridge Loop

100

Nature
Center

P

1

Old Hickory Boulevard

EDWIN
WARNER PARK

254

Gaucho Road

0.8 Continue heading north until you reach an asphalt park road. Use caution in crossing the road and go up five wooden steps to the trail as it enters the woods.

1.0 Reach a T, which is the end of the Cane Connector Trail. Both branches of the T lead to the 4.5-mile Mossy Ridge Loop, and the left branch leads to the 2.0-mile Warner Woods Trail. Backtrack to the trailhead, or extend the hike.

2.0 Arrive back at the trailhead.

2 Radnor Lake State Natural Area: Spillway Trail and Lake Trail

This hike takes you around the lake and through heavy woods containing beech, tulip poplar, and sugar maple. April and May offer birders the best opportunity to see many of the 238 species that frequent the woods and lake.

Start: Spillway Trail trailhead, behind the visitor center
Distance: 3.5-mile clockwise loop
Approximate hiking time: 3 hours
Difficulty: Moderate due to some steep slopes
Trail surface: Dirt, rock
Best season: Year-round
Other trail users: Birders
Canine compatibility: Dogs not permitted
Fees and permits: None required
Schedule: 6:00 a.m. to dark

Maps: USGS: Oak Hill; trail maps available at the visitor center
Trail contact: Manager, Radnor Lake State Natural Area, 1160 Otter Creek Rd., Nashville 37220; (615) 373-3467; www.radnorlake.org
Other: Restrooms and water are available at the visitor center; there is no potable water or restroom on the trail. Take adequate drinking water and use sunscreen and insect repellent. Several sections of the trail have sharp drop-offs, so keep young children in hand. Joggers and cyclists are prohibited on the trail.

Finding the trailhead: From I-65 South in downtown Nashville, exit at Harding Place and go west. Harding Place turns into Battery Lane. Turn left on Granny White Pike and go about 2 miles, then turn left (east) on Otter Creek Road to 1160 Otter Creek Rd., and the visitor center and parking area. *DeLorme Tennessee Atlas & Gazetteer:* Page 53 D5. GPS: N36 03.80 / W86 48.61

The Hike

Start at the trailhead and quickly reach an observation deck—take a moment to look for animals and birds. The lake is not in view, but the lake and the park's 1,200 acres are a magnet for waterbirds. Many species of ducks, including gadwall, American widgeon, and canvasback, spend the winter there.

Reach the spillway bridge on the right and take a short out-and-back to the spillway. The bridge furnishes one of the better views of the lake and affords excellent photo ops. Return to the trail as the Spillway Trail turns into the Lake Trail. At bench 13 make a hard left, heading down to an overlook deck at the edge of the lake. Look for white-tailed deer in this area in the early morning or late afternoon. Listen and look for signs of woodpeckers, especially the yellow-bellied sapsucker. It is medium size, about 8 to 9 inches long, and has a red forehead patch.

The woods are predominantly oak and hickory, but beeches and tulip poplars may also be seen. In the spring look for mountain laurel and elderberries, which are not commonly found in this central basin. Continue south until reaching a T; take the right branch, heading toward the lake. The left branch leads to the 1.5-mile Ganier Ridge Trail.

Cross a bridge near the southeast corner of the lake and bear right. In the spring look for wildflowers, mosses, and ferns growing along the edge of the trail. Continue south until reaching a Y; take the right branch, staying on Lake Trail. Listen for birds singing in the woods, including crested flycatchers and scarlet tanagers.

Follow along a causeway intersecting Otter Creek Road (the park road) and turn right onto the road. The lake is in view to the right. The area between the road and water is a favorite spot for water snakes, including the venomous water moccasin. Turtles and waterbirds, including ducks, are often seen here.

Cross Otter Creek Road to reach the connector trail to the South Cove Trail and South Lake Trail. Thirty-seven steps lead up to this narrow trail that weaves through the woods and up the ridge. Use caution because the right edge of the trail drops sharply down to the road. At bench 51 bear left, heading northwest, and cross a bridge. Reach a Y and take the right branch, continuing on the South Lake Trail. This is one of the most strenuous sections of the hike.

Reach an intersection on the right that has sixteen steps leading down. Go down the steps and cross a bridge with Radnor Lake to the right. Cross another short bridge and immediately bear left, still going generally northwest.

Go down the steps leading to Otter Creek Road and turn left onto Otter Creek Road. Follow the road northwest to the Dam Walkway. Cross the walkway; follow it and cross the spillway bridge, which connects with the Spillway Trail. Turn left onto the Spillway Trail, and backtrack to the visitor center.

Miles and Directions

0.0 Start at the back of the visitor center and follow the boardwalk to the Spillway Trail trailhead.

0.1 Within 0.1 mile reach a T and take the left branch onto the Lake Trail. Reach an observation deck on the right and pass bench 6.

0.4 Pass benches 8 and 10 on the left; Radnor Lake is about 30 feet away. Continue on the trail and cross a bridge; make a hard right and pass bench 12 on the left.

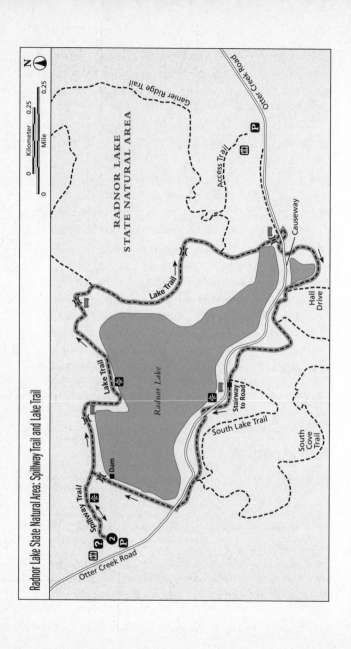

Radnor Lake State Natural Area: Spillway Trail and Lake Trail

RADNOR LAKE
STATE NATURAL AREA

Radnor Lake

Otter Creek Road

Ganier Ridge Trail

Access Trail

Causeway

Hall Drive

Lake Trail

Lake Trail

Dam

Spillway Trail

Otter Creek Road

Stairway to Road

South Lake Trail

South Cove Trail

0   Kilometer   0.25

0   Mile   0.25

N

0.5 Bear left up a slight slope and reach bench 13. Take a hard left toward the lake and an overlook deck. Bear right around the lake.

0.8 Continue following the trail generally east. Pass benches 18, 19, and 20.

0.9 Bear slightly left and pass bench 21. Cross a bridge and then bear hard right, going up a slight slope.

1.1 Reach a T and take the right branch. The left branch leads to the Ganier Ridge Trail. Pass benches 22, 23, and 24. Bear left from bench 24.

1.3 Bear sweeping left and then hard left away from the lake. The lake is not visible.

1.5 Bear slightly to the right and reach a bridge over a dry creek bed. Bear slightly right, and almost immediately reach a Y. Take the right branch, following the Lake Trail.

1.6 Reach a Y and take the right branch, following the Lake Trail. The left branch leads to the Ganier Ridge Trail. Continue following the Lake Trail, bearing slightly left and up passing bench 28.

1.8 Cross a bridge over a swampy area and then pass bench 30. Almost immediately reach Otter Creek Road; follow the road to the right. Radnor Lake is to the right about 5 feet away. Follow the road along the edge of Radnor Lake.

2.0 Pass a road to the left that leads to the Environmental Education Center. Continue following Otter Creek Road.

2.1 Carefully cross Otter Creek Road to the trailhead and steps leading up the hill to the South Cove Trail and South Lake Trail. Climb the steps and follow the South Lake Trail as it heads south. At bench 51 bear left and immediately reach a short wood bridge. Cross the bridge and continue on the South Lake Trail.

2.2 Reach a Y and take the right branch, continuing on the South Lake Trail. This section is one of the most strenuous parts of the trail. Continue following the trail, bearing hard right and then up a moderately steep slope.

2.3 Go down a set of steps and reach a wood bridge. Cross the bridge and follow the trail as it slopes down and passes bench 50.

2.4 Continue following the trail generally northwest and cross a short bridge. Radnor Lake can be seen on the right across Otter Creek Road. Immediately after the bridge, bear left and then right, going slightly uphill.

2.6 Reach steps on the right leading down to Otter Creek Road. Go down the thirty-six steps and turn left onto Otter Creek Road. Radnor Lake is to the right of the road.

2.7 Pass an observation deck that overlooks the lake. Continue following the road, bearing slightly to the left.

2.9 Pass a Y on the left that is a connector for the South Cove Trail and South Lake Trail. Continue on the road.

3.0 Look to the right for the trail across the dam spillway. Cross the road and follow the trail across the Dam Walkway. At the end of the spillway bridge, reach a T and take the left branch to the Spillway Trail. Backtrack to the trailhead and visitor center.

3.5 Arrive back at the trailhead.

3 Ellington Agricultural Center: Eagle Trail and Roberts Walk

Flower lovers will want to spend time in the Bicentennial Iris Garden that's at the end of the Eagle Trail. Circle a ten-acre meadow, whose eastern portion borders Seven Mile Creek, which is a year-round haven for birds. The center is listed as an Official Arboretum by the Nashville Tree Foundation.

Start: Eagle Trail trailhead, near the parking area
Distance: 1.7-mile clockwise loop
Approximate hiking time: 1.5 hours
Difficulty: Easy, due to flat surface
Trail surface: Dirt, grass
Best season: Year-round
Other trail users: Dog walkers, birders; portions of the trail wheelchair and stroller accessible
Canine compatibility: Leashed dogs permitted

Fees and permits: None required
Schedule: Dawn to dusk
Maps: USGS: Antioch; trail maps available at Ellington Agricultural Center and at www.tn.gov /agriculture
Trail contact: Manager, Ellington Agricultural Center, 440 Hogan Rd., Nashville 37220; (615) 837-5103; www.tn.gov /agriculture
Other: There is no potable water or restrooms on the trail. Take adequate drinking water and use sunscreen and insect repellent.

Finding the trailhead: From the south side of Nashville, take I-40 East/I-65 South via the ramp on the left toward Knoxville. Go 0.9 mile, then merge onto I-65 South toward Huntsville via exit 210 and proceed 4.3 miles. Take TN 255 at exit 78B and go 0.2 mile. Make a slight right onto Harding Place/TN 255, then turn left onto Franklin Road (US 31/TN 6). Turn left onto Hogan Road, then turn left at 440

Hogan Rd. and proceed to the parking area. *Note:* Hogan Road ends at the Ellington Agricultural Center's front gate. *DeLorme Tennessee Atlas & Gazetteer:* Page 53 D5. GPS: N36 03.74 / W86 44.77

The Hike

This hike passes woodlands, meadows, and creeks throughout a 207-acre area that hosts 124 bird species. Start at the Eagle Trail trailhead, adjoining the parking area, and head west. The Eagle Trail leads through the Iris Garden and connects to Roberts Walk. Portions of the trail are wheelchair and stroller accessible.

Follow the 400-foot-long Eagle Trail as it heads downhill into the Bicentennial Iris Garden. These are formal gardens with benches and flowing water that create a visual display not normally seen on a hike. Reach the ROBERTS WALK sign and follow the mulched path on the left side of the road. The Agricultural Center buildings are situated on the top of the hill. Bend right and cross over two sections of paved brick.

The trail leads into a large open meadow that covers ten acres. Follow the trail along the park boundary, bordered on the left by Seven Mile Creek. Reach a path on the left that leads down to the creek and small gurgling rapids that create a great photo op. Watch for purple martins swooping low over the meadow on the right, scooping up insects.

Several power transmission posts at the north end of the meadow furnish platforms for red-tailed hawks to watch for unsuspecting prey, including birds, small mammals, and snakes. Bear right at the transmission posts, heading into the woods. Many birds can be heard and seen, including sparrows, yellowthroats, and the small but beautiful indigo bunting. The Agricultural Center boundary fence is on the left and the unseen campus on the right.

Continue following the trail through the woods as it slopes gradually up toward the hilltop. Large mature trees, including sugar maple, black walnut, and hackberry, are favorites for migrating warblers, especially during the spring. This portion of the hike is very relaxing and is a good spot to add an extra dimension to the hike by identifying birds or trees with the help of a guidebook.

Follow along the Agricultural Center boundary fence, which is on the left. Pass a path on the right that leads through some shrubs to the campus. This path may be taken to shorten the hike. Reach two posts in the center of the trail and just beyond them an Agricultural Center road. Cross the road and immediately turn right onto the Campus Connector path, which is wheelchair and stroller accessible. It heads slightly up, along the edge of the campus on the left. Follow the path as it turns left across a parking area and various campus buildings, including the Tennessee Agriculture Museum and several old log structures. This is a good spot for history buffs to spend some time before reaching the parking area for the Eagle Trail and ending the hike.

Miles and Directions

0.0 Start at the Eagle Trail trailhead, near the parking area, and head west.

0.1 Pass through the Iris Garden on the very short Eagle Trail, leading to the Roberts Walk trailhead. Go left, heading northwest on the trail paralleling the asphalt road.

0.3 Go down and then up a bricked area. The Agricultural Center buildings are to the right but nearly hidden by a hill. Bear northeast, and pass the Campus Connector path on the right.

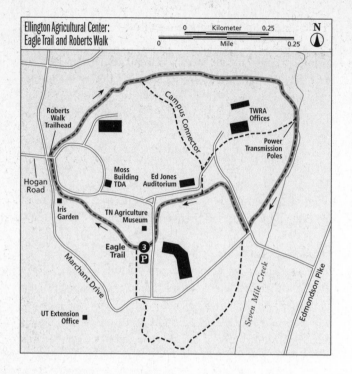

Ellington Agricultural Center:
Eagle Trail and Roberts Walk

0   Kilometer   0.25
0   Mile   0.25

N

Roberts
Walk
Trailhead

TWRA
Offices

Campus Connector

Power
Transmission
Poles

Hogan
Road

Moss
Building
TDA

Ed Jones
Auditorium

Iris
Garden

TN Agriculture
Museum

Eagle
Trail

3
P

Marchant Drive

Seven Mile Creek

Edmondson Pike

UT Extension
Office

0.5 Reach a ten-acre meadow, with Seven Mile Creek on the left. Continue following the trail until it reaches a path on the left that leads to the creek. Take this short out-and-back to explore the rapids.

0.7 Continue following the trail along the creek, heading northeast and toward a line of power transmission poles.

0.9 Reach the transmission poles and make a hard right, heading east. Heavy woods are on the left and the meadow is on the right. Follow the trail for about 200 feet along the transmission poles and enter the woods.

1.2 Continue following the trail east then south and slightly up. An Agricultural Center boundary fence is on the left. Pass a path on the right that leads to the campus and can be taken to shorten the hike.

1.3 Reach two posts in the center of the trail and then an Agriculture Center road. Cross the road and immediately turn right onto the Campus Connector path, which heads west and slightly up along the edge of the campus on the left. Follow the path as it turns left, passing various campus buildings.

1.7 Arrive back at the trailhead and parking area.

4 Nashville Greenway: Shelby Bottoms Nature Trail

A portion of this trail parallels the Cumberland River. This area features bottomland, hardwood forests, open fields, and wetlands. The long pedestrian bridge over the Cumberland River offers great views of the river. This is a good hike for a family with young children.

Start: The unmarked trailhead at the east side of the parking area at Two Rivers Park
Distance: 2.2-mile out-and-back
Approximate hiking time: 1 hour
Difficulty: Easy
Trail surface: Asphalt
Best season: Year-round
Other trail users: Joggers, dog walkers, bicyclists, strollers, wheelchairs
Canine compatibility: Leashed dogs permitted

Fees and permits: None required
Schedule: 8:00 a.m. to 5:00 p.m.
Maps: USGS: Nashville East; maps available at www.nashville .gov/parks/wpnc
Trail contact: www.nashville .gov/parks/wpnc
Other: A portable toilet is available at the parking area. There is no potable water or restrooms on the trail.

Finding the trailhead: From the southwest side of Nashville, take I-40 East via the ramp on the left toward Knoxville. Go 6 miles, then merge onto Briley Parkway via exit 215B and proceed 1.9 miles. Take the Lebanon Pike/US 70 exit (exit 8) toward Donelson and go 0.3 mile. Turn right on Lebanon Pike/US 70 and proceed 0.3 mile. Turn left on McGavock Pike and go 1.1 miles to 3150 McGavock Pike. Turn into Two Rivers Park and proceed to the parking area and

kiosk for the trail. *DeLorme Tennessee Atlas & Gazetteer:* Page 53
C5. GPS: N36 11.52 / W86 40.67

The Hike

This multiuse trail is in the 810-acre Shelby Bottoms
Greenway and Nature Park. This is a linear park, which
means all hikes are out and back. Shelby Park is at the southern terminus, and residential areas are on the west side. The
Cumberland River borders the east side. Benches are placed
appropriately along the trail. This area is said to be one of
the best birding areas in Nashville.

Start at the unmarked trailhead on the east side of the
parking area in Two Rivers Park and head north. This
portion of the trail is "busy" with highways and power
lines. In less than 0.3 mile bear hard left, heading west, and
go through two highway underpasses and reach the long
pedestrian bridge over the Cumberland. Cross the bridge
and make a hard left at the end of the bridge, heading
southwest. Follow the trail as it heads up a small hill to an
observation area.

Follow the trail down the hill to rejoin the main trail.
Notice the pond west of the hill. The trail heads southwest,
with the Cumberland on the left. Woods, including hickories, beech, elm, and various species of oak, furnish great
habitat for birds and small mammals. There are also some
small stands of native cane near the river. In the spring listen
and watch for warblers. Nearly all warblers seen in Tennessee have been seen here. Listen and look for the white-eyed
vireo, which breeds here. This is a small bird, colored gray-
ish olive on its upper body and white below. The eyes are
circled by a yellow line, which look like spectacles. It likes
to be in the shrubbery and undergrowth.

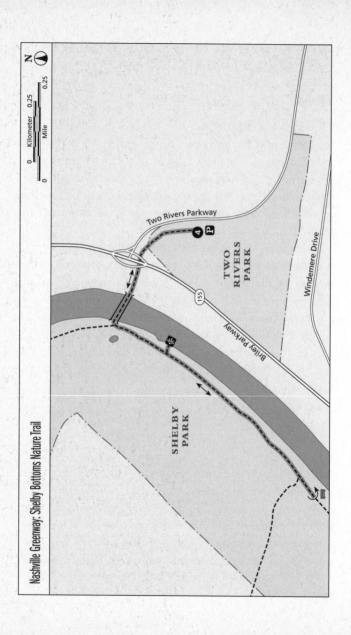

Nashville Greenway: Shelby Bottoms Nature Trail

N

0   0.25   Kilometer
0   0.25   Mile

Two Rivers Parkway

TWO
RIVERS
PARK

Windemere Drive

155

Briley Parkway

SHELBY
PARK

Continue southwest, with the river on the left. Trees sometimes block the view of the river. There are several small paths that lead to overlooks on the river's edge. Limestone rocks edge portions of the river. The river is generally 8 feet or more below the trail. Notice the small patches of native cane that grow near the water. Cross a bridge over a narrow seasonal creek and continue heading southwest. At just over 1.0 mile, reach a sign on the right with information and a map. There is a bench that is partially shaded. It is 2.5 miles, continuing southwest, to Shelby Park. This is a good spot to rest a moment and then backtrack northeast to the bridge. Notice things on the way back that you may not have seen earlier. End the hike back at the trailhead.

Miles and Directions

0.0 Start at the unmarked Shelby Bottoms Greenway Trail trailhead, at the east side of the Two Rivers Park parking area. Turn left onto the asphalt trail and head north.

0.2 Continue north on the trail toward the underpass at Briley Parkway.

0.3 Follow the trail as it veers left (west) and then proceed through the underpasses for Briley Parkway and Two Rivers Parkway.

0.4 Cross the pedestrian bridge over the Cumberland River. Follow the trail up and around an observation area. Turn right back onto the trail and head southwest, The river is on the left.

0.5 Pass a pond on the right, about 40 feet away. Reach a T and take the left branch, still heading southwest.

0.7 Continue following the trail until you reach a path that comes in from the right. Take a short out-and-back to an overlook at the river's edge. Return to the trail and continue southwest.

0.9 Cross a bridge over a narrow seasonal creek. Continue following the trail as it veers right, left, and back right, still heading southwest.

1.1 Reach a bench and sign with a trail map. Stop and backtrack to the trailhead. The trail continues on to Shelby Park.

2.2 Arrive back at the trailhead.

5 Brentwood Greenway: River Park Trail

This in-city hike offers a variety of changing scenes to pique your interest. Cross bridges and follow the Little Harpeth River. Sometimes woods and wild honeysuckle edge the trail; other times, soccer fields or tennis courts. This is an excellent hike for families with young children.

Start: The unmarked River Park Trail trailhead, at the northeast side of the parking area

Distance: 2.7-mile out-and-back

Approximate hiking time: 1.5 hours

Difficulty: Easy, due to flat paved trail

Trail surface: Asphalt

Best season: Sept-June

Other trail users: Joggers, bicyclists, skateboarders, dog walkers, strollers, wheelchairs

Canine compatibility: Leashed dogs permitted

Fees and permits: None required

Schedule: Dawn to dusk

Maps: USGS: Franklin; trail maps available at the Brentwood Parks and recreation Department

Trail contact: Brentwood Parks and Recreation Department, 1750 General George Patton Dr., Brentwood 37027; (615) 371-0080; www.brentwood-tn.org

Other: Water and restrooms available near the parking area

Finding the trailhead: From the south side of Nashville, take I-40 East via the ramp on the left toward Knoxville and go 0.9 mile. Merge onto I-65 South via exit 210 toward Huntsville and go 10.9 miles. Take TN 253, exit 71, toward Brentwood and go 0.4 mile. Turn left onto Concord Road and go 0.6 mile, then turn right onto Knox Valley Drive and proceed 0.2 mile to 1200 Knox Valley Dr. in Brentwood. Follow the park road to the parking area and trailhead. *DeLorme Tennessee Atlas & Gazetteer:* Page 53 D5. GPS: N35 59.70 / W86 47.25

The Hike

This hike may represent the in-city hiking of the future. The trail is located in Brentwood's River Park and is part of the Brentwood Greenway system. Water fountains, restrooms, a playground, a shelter, and picnic tables are adjacent to the parking area. These can be an incentive to hikers with young children. The Little Harpeth River borders much of the River Park Trail.

Begin your hike at the unmarked River Park Trail trailhead, at the east side of the parking area. Pass a sign that reads ENTERING RIVER PARK BIKEWAY, then immediately cross a bridge over the Little Harpeth River and turn right, heading south. There is a large map board at the end of the bridge. The Brentwood YMCA and soccer fields are to the left. Continue following the trail along the river, which is on the right.

The trail bends right and then reaches a walk-around containing a picnic table. The river is on the right but is not visible. Pass a two-bench shelter (a small covered shelter with back-to-back benches), a signature feature of this park. Notice the fence on the left, enclosing a horse pasture—Tennesseans love their horses. A large group of limestone blocks is scattered in the clearing on the right. Follow the trail as it gets within 6 feet of the river. This is a very picturesque section, creating a great opportunity for photos.

Reach a short loop around a two-sided covered shelter. Take either branch, since they rejoin after the shelter. Within 250 feet reach a bench at the river's edge, facing the water. Honeysuckle bushes and large sycamore trees, which can grow 10 feet a year, line the river's edge. A sign behind the bench gives information about the Little Harpeth River.

In the spring and early summer, black-eyed Susans, Queen Anne's lace, and orange-flowering trumpet vines are all in vibrant bloom. Return to the trail and pass a lighted emergency call box.

Catch a glimpse of the river, about 10 feet away. Hardwood trees line the riverbank. As the trail draws closer to the river, listen for the soft gurgling of rapids. The tree canopy is open, affording little shade. Listen for birds while passing marker post 8, especially the eastern phoebe. This 7-inch-long bird is easily identified by its distinctive song, a harsh emphatic *fee bee*. It is brownish gray on its upper body and white on its belly.

Pass marker post 9 and a two-bench covered shelter and continue following the trail as it bends right and reaches a T. Take the left branch, still heading generally south. The right branch leads to Wikle Road. Continue following the trail until reaching a marker that states TURNAROUND. Just ahead is the tunnel under Wilson Pike and the CSX railroad tracks that lead to Crockett Park. This is a good spot to turn around and backtrack to the trailhead.

Miles and Directions

0.0 Start at the unmarked River Park Trail trailhead at the northeast edge of the parking area.

0.1 Immediately cross a bridge over the Little Harpeth River and turn right, heading south. There is a large map board at the end of the bridge. Follow the trail along the river.

0.3 Pass several trail marker posts and a three-rail wood pasture fence on the left. Bear left; the river is about 8 feet away on the right.

0.5 Continue following the trail generally south and reach a narrow Y. The left and right branches form a loop around a

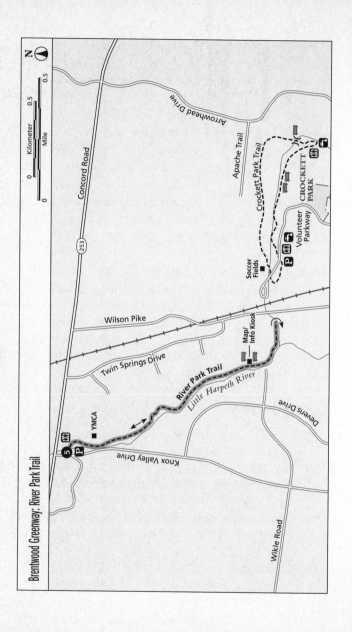

Brentwood Greenway: River Park Trail

N

Kilometer
0   0.5

Mile
0   0.5

Concord Road

253

Arrowhead Drive

Apache Trail

Crockett Park Trail

CROCKETT PARK

Volunteer Parkway

Soccer Fields

P

Wilson Pike

Twin Springs Drive

Map/ Info Kiosk

River Park Trail

Little Harpeth River

Devens Drive

Knox Valley Drive

YMCA

P

Wikle Road

shelter that has a bench. Follow either branch, since they meet and rejoin the trail.

0.7 Pass an emergency call box on the left. Continue generally south and pass marker posts 6 and 7. Bend left, temporarily heading west.

0.9 Cross a drainage culvert and bear left and then right, passing a path leading to the river, which is about 50 feet away. Pass marker post 9 and a covered shelter on the left.

1.0 Continue following the trail as it gets nearer the river. The trail bends right and reaches a T. Take the left branch along the Little Harpeth River, heading generally south. The right branch leads to Wikle Road.

1.2 Reach a Y and take the left branch. The right branch is a path to Ravenwood High School.

1.4 Bear left toward the Wilson Pike and railroad underpass. Reach a sign on the right that says TURNAROUND. Continue on to investigate the underpass and then backtrack to the trailhead.

2.7 Arrive back at the trailhead.

6 Brentwood: Deerwood Arboretum Trail

This hike is for tree lovers, pond enthusiasts, and those wanting a bit of solitude. Overlooks and paths to the Little Harpeth River and nature ponds provide a bit of adventure for young children. The paved flat trail is easily navigated with those who use wheelchairs or have mobility problems.

Start: Deerwood Arboretum Trail trailhead, adjacent to the northeast side of the parking area
Distance: 1.4-mile clockwise loop
Approximate hiking time: 1.5 hours
Difficulty: Easy, due to flat paved trail
Trail surface: Asphalt
Best season: Year-round
Other trail users: Joggers, bicyclist, skaters, dog walkers, strollers, and wheelchairs

Canine compatibility: Leashed dogs permitted
Fees and permits: None required
Schedule: Dawn to dusk
Maps: USGS: Oak Hill; trail maps available at the Brentwood Parks and Recreation Department
Trail contacts: Brentwood Parks and Recreation Department, 1750 General George Patton Dr., Brentwood 37027; (615) 371-0080; www.brentwood-tn.org
Other: No potable water on the trail

Finding the trailhead: From the south side of Nashville, take I-40 East via the ramp on the left toward Knoxville and go 0.9 mile. Merge onto I-65 via exit 210 toward Huntsville and go 7.9 miles. Merge onto Old Hickory Boulevard via exit 74B toward Brentwood, and then turn left onto Granny White Pike after 0.5 mile and go 1.2 miles. Turn right onto Belle Rive Drive and go 1.2 miles; Belle Rive Drive becomes Johnson Chapel Road. Follow Johnson Chapel Road for 0.3 mile and turn right onto Deerwood Lane and proceed 0.1 mile to 320 Deerwood Lane, which is on the right, into Deerwood

Arboretum. *DeLorme Tennessee Atlas & Gazetteer:* Page 53 D5. GPS: N36 2.131 / W86 47.252

The Hike

Obtain a copy of the Deerwood Arboretum *Tree Identification Trail Guide,* because it contains the ID numbers posted on some trees that identify the species. There is a kiosk with a large map board at the trailhead. The area has many trees, two ponds, and the Little Harpeth River, making it ideal habitat for birds and small mammals.

From the trailhead follow a very short connector trail to a T and take the right branch. Almost immediately pass a tree on the right with ID sign #3, which identifies the tree as a white ash. Emergency call box #900 is located on the left side of the trail. A pond can be seen on the other side of the road.

Cross Deerwood Lane, which is the "park road" and leads to the parking area. Reach a Y and take the right branch. There is a bench in the fork of the Y, and the Little Harpeth River can be seen to the rear of the bench. This is a good spot to sit a minute and check out the bald cypress tree (ID sign #7) alongside the bench. This large tree thrives in very wet, swampy soils. It is sometimes called "the eternal wood" due to its resistance to decay. Notice the knobby exposed roots.

At 0.5 mile, reach a gravel path on the left that leads to the river. Go down a few steps to the riverbank and investigate the amphibian life. Wildflowers fill this area in the spring. Return and follow the trail for 0.3 mile until reaching a dirt path on the right. Take the path to a clearing, east of the pond. There are benches and flat limestone rocks to sit on. Walking around the perimeter of the pond and

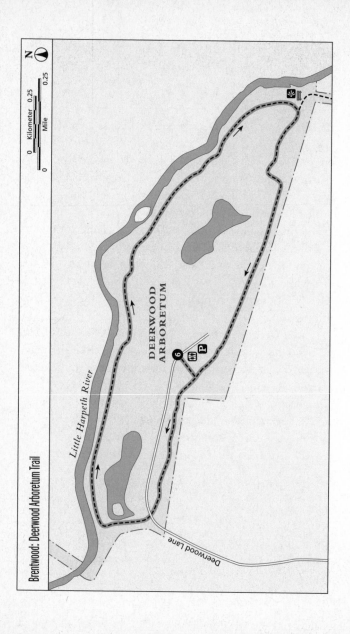

Brentwood: Deerwood Arboretum Trail

DEERWOOD
ARBORETUM

Little Harpeth River

Deerwood Lane

N

0   Kilometer   0.25

0   Mile   0.25

exploring the various plants are the high points of the hike. Two fountains in the pond furnish circulation and aeration.

Return to the trail and in about 500 feet reach a T; take the left branch, passing a sign that states, LITTLE HARPETH RIVER VIEW. A path on the left leads to an overlook, 7 feet above the river. Investigate the overlook and return to the trail. Almost immediately reach a kiosk that has a large map of the arboretum. At this point the arboretum trail ends and joins a greenway trail that leads out of the arboretum. Backtrack to the previous T and take the left branch and head northwest.

Continue hiking northwest, passing the pond you visited earlier. Numerous tree ID signs are along the edge of the trail. Eastern red cedar, Osage orange, and sassafras trees are identified along the side of the trail. Reach the T near the trailhead and take the right branch to end the hike.

Miles and Directions

0.0 Start at the Arboretum Trail trailhead, adjoining the south side of the parking area. A very short connector trail leads to a T. Take the right branch heading west to northwest.

0.1 Continue following the trail northwest, passing numerous trees with ID signs. Notice a pond across Deerwood Lane to the northeast.

0.2 Pass several trees with ID signs on the right. Deerwood Lane is on the right, and a low mound hides the pond. Continue following the trail and cross Deerwood Lane.

0.3 The Little Harpeth River can be seen on the left. Tree ID sign #32 identifying a chinquapin oak is on the left. Continue following the trail northeast, with the river on the left.

0.4 Follow the trail northeast, passing the restrooms to the far right. Continue heading east on the paved trail.

0.5 Bear slightly left at the tree with ID sign #43 heading east by northeast. In 20 feet take the gravel path to the river. Investigate the river's edge and return to the main trail, heading east by southeast.

0.7 Reach a dirt path on the left behind a bench. Tree ID sign #33 is on the right. Take the path that ends about 7 feet above the river. Return to the trail and head southeast.

0.8 Bear slightly right, then left and back right, still heading southeast. Reach a 5-foot-wide dirt path on the right. Take the path to a mowed area and then the pond. Investigate the pond by walking around the perimeter.

1.0 Return to the main trail via the dirt path and turn right, heading nearly south. The river is about 15 feet away on the left. Continue while heading southeast.

1.1 Reach a T and take the left branch. This leads to a river overlook. There is a kiosk on the right with a map of the arboretum. The trail joins another trail that leaves the arboretum. Backtrack 200 feet to the previous T and take the left branch, heading northwest.

1.2 Reach tree ID sign #26 on the right and take a hard right. The trail heads slightly up, still heading northwest.

1.4 Reach the T and take right branch to arrive back at the trailhead.

7 Pinkerton Park: Exercise Loop Trail

This wide paved trail serves hikers, joggers, dog walkers, wheelchairs, strollers, and those seeking a fitness trail. It winds between trees, shrubbery, and mowed areas, with exercise stations interspersed along the way. A large playground may be an attraction for families with young children.

Start: The unmarked Exercise Loop Trail trailhead, near the Pinkerton Park parking area
Distance: 1.1-mile clockwise loop
Approximate hiking time: 1 hour, taking time to participate in exercise stations
Difficulty: Easy
Trail surface: Asphalt and concrete
Best season: Year-round
Other trail users: Joggers, dog walkers, strollers, wheelchairs, people using fitness stations

Canine compatibility: Leashed dogs permitted
Fees and permits: None required
Schedule: Dawn to dusk
Maps: USGS: Franklin; no trail maps available
Trail contacts: Franklin Parks and Recreation, 705 Boyd Mill Ave., Franklin 37064; (615) 790-5885; www.wcparksandrec .com
Other: Water and restrooms available in Pinkerton Park

Finding the trailhead: From the south side of Nashville, take I-40 East via the ramp on the left toward Knoxville and go 0.9 mile. Merge onto I-65 South, via exit 210, toward Huntsville, and go 16.9 miles. Take TN 96, exit 65, toward Franklin and go 0.2 mile. Turn right onto Murfreesboro Road and go 2.2 miles to 405 Murfreesboro Rd. in Franklin on the right. Proceed to the parking area. *DeLorme Tennessee Atlas & Gazetteer:* Page 35 A5. GPS: N35 55.820 / W86 51.730

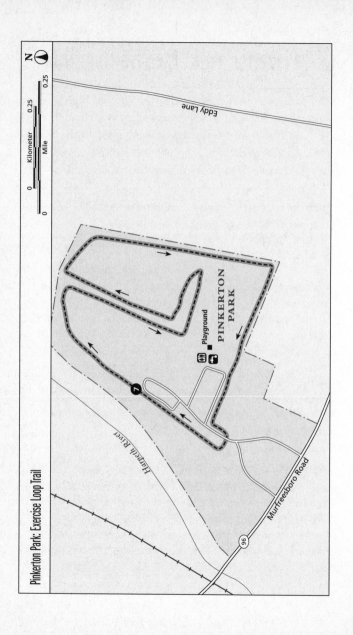

Pinkerton Park: Exercise Loop Trail

PINKERTON PARK

Playground

Harpeth River

Eddy Lane

Murfreesboro Road

96

N

Kilometer   0   0.25

Mile   0   0.25

7

The Hike

Start at the unmarked paved multiuse Exercise Loop Trail trailhead, adjacent to the parking area. The Tinkerbell playground, restrooms, and a water fountain are to the right. Picnic tables and grills are scattered throughout the park. The playground may be an incentive for families with young children. The Harpeth River, which cannot be seen, borders the northwest leg of the trail. All areas within Pinkerton Park are mowed.

Follow the asphalt and sometimes concrete clockwise loop trail as it heads south, then north, again south, then west, and finishes northeast. All these turns happen within a mile. There is a sign near the beginning of the trail that states, THIS IS PART OF THE LIFE TRAIL. The Life Trail is a well-designed series of exercise stations along its edge. Single rows of mature hardwoods, including oak and maple, are along the edges of the trail. Swings and benches are placed along both sides of the trail. Sometimes the branches of these trees form an arch, creating a pleasant area of shade. Soccer fields can be seen to the left.

The hike furnishes the opportunity to hear and see birds and squirrels. The river and shrubs and trees provide good habitat. Major attractions for this wildlife are the crumbs and droppings of picnickers. At 0.25 mile, the trail doubles back on itself. This is a good spot to listen and look for birds, which have become accustomed to hikers. In the spring watch for the common goldfinch. It is a small bird, 5 to 5½ inches long, smaller than a sparrow. It is easy to identify because it is the only small yellow bird with black wings. It has a stout bill, common to finches. Their flight is erratic. When they are flying, listen for their simple song of a long-sustained *ti-dee-di-di*. Add a dimension to the hike by having a bird guide.

Continue following the trail as it winds through trees and exercise stations adjoining the trail. Dog refuse bags are placed on posts around the trail. Pass a picnic area with benches and grills, follow along the edge of the parking area to the unmarked trailhead, and end the hike.

Miles and Directions

No Miles and Directions are given for this hike. The trail is paved, in view, and surrounded by a children's playground, shelter, restrooms, picnic tables, and benches.

8 Pinkerton Park: Fort Granger Trail

Civil War buffs will enjoy this hike that leads to a 40-foot-high bluff above the Harpeth River, overlooking Franklin. Stairs and a boardwalk assist in the hike up the steep hillside to the location of the fort. The fort was constructed in 1863 by Union soldiers.

Start: Fort Granger Trail trailhead, adjacent to the parking area

Distance: 1.1-mile lollipop

Approximate hiking time: 1 hour, to allow time to read information signs

Difficulty: Easy

Trail surface: Dirt, grass

Best season: Year-round

Other trail users: Joggers, dog walkers

Canine compatibility: Leashed dogs permitted

Fees and permits: None required

Schedule: Dawn to dusk

Maps: USGS: Franklin; no trail map available

Trail contact: Franklin Parks and Recreation, 705 Boyd Mill Ave., Franklin 37064; (615) 790-5885; www.wcparksandrec.com

Other: Water and restrooms available in Pinkerton Park

Finding the trailhead: From the south side of Nashville, take I-40 East via the ramp on the left toward Knoxville and go 0.9 mile. Merge onto I-65 South via exit 210 toward Huntsville and go 16.9 miles. Take TN 96, exit 65, toward Franklin and go 0.2 mile. Turn right onto Murfreesboro Road and go 2.2 miles to 405 Murfreesboro Rd., Franklin, on the right. Proceed to the parking area. *DeLorme Tennessee Atlas & Gazetteer:* Page 37 A5. GPS: N35 55.35 / W86 51.73

The Hike

Hikers interested in learning about a Union fort built to protect Franklin during the Civil War will appreciate this hike.

The fort is gone, but informational signs tell where buildings were located, the placement of guns, and other interesting data. The fort was an earthwork structure, 781 feet long and 346 feet wide, covering nearly twelve acres. The sentry/observation trail on the edge of the bluff is intact, furnishing a view down the hill toward Franklin. Fort Granger is located on 40-foot-high Figuer's Bluff, above the Harpeth River overlooking Franklin. This bluff joins the north side of Pinkerton Park. The nearly 8,000 soldiers stationed at the fort during the Battle of Franklin on November 30, 1864, had ringside seats to one of the bloodiest battles of the Civil War.

Follow the sidewalk north from the parking area to the FORT GRANGER sign, located near the Y at the trailhead. Take the left branch down a slight slope and immediately reach a bridge crossing a meander of the Harpeth River. The area is mowed, and there are electric utility lines overhead. Reach a clearing 150 feet wide by 300 feet deep and continue following the narrow dirt trail across the clearing. Pass the Outdoor Learning Center and immediately reach a steep set of steps, with limestone outcrops along and below them. Continue up the steps and reach a boardwalk. The boardwalk is long, with a set of steps. There is a large observation area with views of trees and utility power lines.

Exit the boardwalk by a set of steps leading to the former sentry path adjoining Fort Granger along the top of the bluff. During the battle the hill overlooking Franklin was bare, but now trees and undergrowth cover it. Follow this path while trying to imagine what it was like being a soldier on sentry duty. Follow to the right and up a small incline to the grounds of the fort. There is no trail through the fort area, so just go from information sign to information sign, eventually heading back toward the boardwalk.

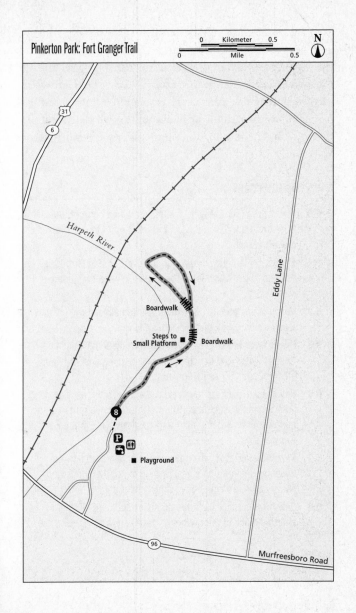

Pinkerton Park: Fort Granger Trail

0   Kilometer   0.5
0   Mile   0.5

N

31
6

Harpeth River

Eddy Lane

Boardwalk

Steps to
Small Platform

Boardwalk

8

P

■ Playground

96

Murfreesboro Road

One of the most interesting signs discusses Fort Granger's history. It notes there was a 9,000-gallon cistern near the sign—that's a lot of water, since many rural homes today consider a 500-gallon cistern very large. Hardwood trees, including oak and maple, are scattered throughout the fort grounds, furnishing small amounts of shade. Continue investigating the information signs until reaching the boardwalk and backtracking to the trailhead.

Miles and Directions

0.0 Start at the Fort Granger Trail trailhead, just north of the Pinkerton Park parking area, and head north to the Y; take the left branch.

0.1 Almost immediately cross a bridge over a meander of the Harpeth River, which is on the left. Follow the trail, heading northeast.

0.2 Reach stairs leading up a steep hill and almost immediately reach a boardwalk that overlooks the area.

0.3 Go up another set of stairs, which include some limestone "steps." There is a bench at the end of the steps. Continue following the trail as it veers north.

0.5 Reach the top of the bluff and a Y and take the right branch. Fort Granger was situated to the right. Continue following the narrow trail as it bears right and up a small hill to the Fort Granger site.

0.7 Reach the fort site, which does not contain a trail. Investigate the information signs, moving north, then east, and finally south, walking back to the boardwalk.

0.8 Reach the boardwalk at the southern boundary of the fort, and backtrack to the trailhead. Use caution going down the stairs.

1.1 Arrive back at the trailhead.

9 Franklin Greenway: Jim Warren Park Trail

This hike is for those who enjoy the sun and a good exercise trail. The paved multiuse trail weaves along baseball and soccer fields. The hike crosses park roads and parking areas. The trail is wheelchair and stroller accessible. Franklin is 20 miles south of Nashville.

Start: The unmarked trailhead adjoining the park headquarters
Distance: 1.2-mile clockwise loop
Approximate hiking time: 1 hour
Difficulty: Easy
Trail surface: Asphalt, concrete
Best season: Year-round
Other trail users: Joggers, dog walkers, bicyclists, strollers, wheelchairs
Canine compatibility: Leashed dogs permitted

Fees and permits: None required
Schedule: Dawn to dusk
Maps: USGS: Leipers Fork; no trail maps available
Trail contacts: Franklin Parks and Recreation, 705 Boyd Mill Ave., Franklin 37064; (615) 790-5885; www.wcparksandrec .com
Other: Water fountains and restrooms available in various areas of the park

Finding the trailhead: From the south side of Nashville, take I-40 East via the ramp on the left toward Knoxville and go 0.9 mile. Merge onto I-65 South, via exit 210, toward Huntsville and go 16.9 miles. Take TN 96, exit 65, toward Franklin and go 0.2 mile. Turn right onto Murfreesboro Road and go 2.2 miles to 405 Murfreesboro Rd., Franklin, on the right. Proceed to the parking area. *DeLorme Tennessee Atlas & Gazetteer:* Page 37 A5. GPS: N35 55.207 / W86 53.309

The Hike

This hike in Jim Warren Park may be the prototype of future in-city hikes. It offers 2.5 miles of wide paved trails suitable for hikers, bikers, skaters, wheelchairs, strollers, and dog walkers. Water fountains are placed around the park, and restrooms are located near one of the parking areas. Other amenities include numerous sports fields, a shelter, picnic tables, and a playground. All of these amenities are inviting to hikers with young children. One of the downsides is that the trails are crowded on the weekend.

Start at the unmarked trailhead along the park road and near the park headquarters and head west. Other than birds and squirrels, there is virtually no wildlife. A few birds can be heard, and scattered trees furnish some shade. Follow the trail as it bears left, right, and back left. Pass some tennis courts on the right. After 0.1 mile, bear hard right, heading north, and in less than a football field turn hard left, heading west. Follow the trail as it is bordered on the left by privacy fences, shielding residences.

Pass a red maintenance building on the right. In spring watch for young squirrels playfully chasing each other up and down trees. In fall watch for squirrels as they gather nuts to bury them for use in the winter. Many of these nuts will not be found, and they provide future trees for the park. Evenly spaced pine trees form a line on the left edge of the trail. Pass the Franklin Cowboys football field and service buildings and take the left branch of the Y. Head north toward Old Boyd Mill Pike Road, which serves as the park boundary. Follow along the road heading east for the length of a football field and make a hard right, heading south for about 300 feet, and then make a hard left, heading east.

Continue following the trail east. Listen and watch for birds, which have become accustomed to people. Field sparrows are common. They are a small bird with a reddish crown and a noticeable white eye ring and bright pink bill. The pink bill is the key identifier. Look for them in clearings and adjoining woods. They cluster in groups on the ground but do not live in open fields. They can be seen year-round. Follow the asphalt trail as it crosses the park road and leads through parking areas and playing fields. End the hike at the unmarked trailhead.

Miles and Directions

0.0 Start at the unmarked Jim Warren Park Trail trailhead, adjacent to the park headquarters, and head west.

0.1 Follow the trail west until it makes a hard right, heading north. Follow the trail north for 250 feet and then make a hard left, heading west.

0.4 Reach a Y and take the left branch. Make a hard right, heading north toward Old Boyd Mill Road, which is the park boundary.

0.55 Reach Old Boyd Mill Road and follow the trail as it makes a hard right, heading east for the length of a football field. Make a hard right, heading south, for 300 feet and make a hard left, heading east.

0.6 Bear right, pass a JIM WARREN PARK sign on the left. Walk along a fence and the park entrance road. Lighted soccer and ball fields are on several sides.

0.7 Pass a football field, bleachers, and several small buildings used by the Franklin Cowboys football team. Cross the park road and parking lot and pick up the trail. A few park buildings are straight ahead.

0.8 Pass the Franklin Cowboys football complex. Follow the trail as it crosses the park road and through a parking area.

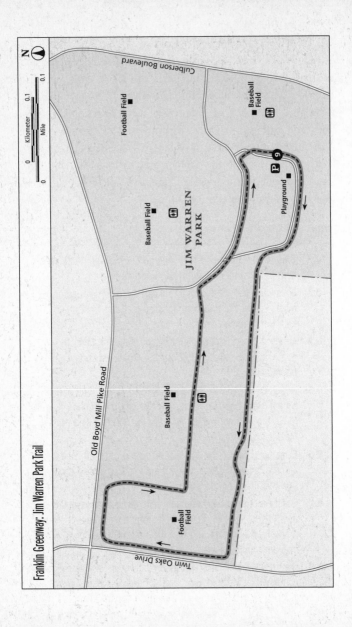

Franklin Greenway: Jim Warren Park Trail

N

Kilometer

Mile

0   0.1

0   0.1

Culberson Boulevard

Old Boyd Mill Pike Road

Twin Oaks Drive

JIM WARREN PARK

Football Field

Baseball Field

Baseball Field

Baseball Field

Football Field

Playground

P

9

Reach the park road and follow it around playing fields, bearing left.

1.0 Follow the trail, bearing left and then right, and heading east. Pass Field 7 on the left and then Field 9, also on the left. Continue toward the trailhead, which is in view.

1.2 Arrive back at the unmarked trailhead.

10 Natchez Trace: Garrison Creek Trail and Overlook Trail

This hike is for those who love history and hilly woods. A short portion of the trail follows the original Natchez Trace that went from Nashville to Natchez, Mississippi. Join and follow the Overlook Branch to a sweeping view of the area. Leipers Fork is 26 miles southwest of Nashville.

Start: Garrison Creek Trail trailhead, just behind the shelter on the east side of the parking area
Distance: 1.6-mile clockwise loop, combining sections of Garrison Creek Trail and the Overlook Trail
Approximate hiking time: 1 hour
Difficulty: Easy
Trail surface: Gravel, dirt
Best season: Year-round
Other trail users: Dog walkers and equestrians
Canine compatibility: Leashed dogs allowed
Fees and permits: None required
Schedule: Dawn to dusk
Maps: USGS: Theta; maps available at trailhead
Trail contacts: National Park Service, Natchez Trace Trail, 2680 Natchez Trace Parkway, Tupelo, MS 38804; (800) 305-7417
Other: Restrooms and water fountains available at the shelter adjoining the parking area

Finding the trailhead: From the south side of Nashville, take I-40 West for 2.6 miles. Merge onto I-440 East, via exit 206, heading toward Knoxville for 2.5 miles. Take US 431 South, via exit 3, and go 0.4 mile. Make a slight right onto 21st Avenue/US 431/TN 106 and follow US 431/TN 106 for 9.4 miles. Turn right on TN 46 and follow Natchez Trace Parkway for less than 2 miles to mile marker 427.6 and turn left into Garrison Creek parking area. *DeLorme Tennessee Atlas & Gazetteer:* Page 36 A3. GPS: N35 52.423 / W87 1.925

The Hike

This 1.6-mile trail that combines the Garrison Creek and Overlook Trail contains a short section of the original Natchez Trace Trail that went from Nashville to Natchez, Mississippi. Garrison Creek was named for a garrison of soldiers who were stationed nearby during the 1800s. This section of the trail allows equestrians, so step carefully.

Start the hike at the Garrison Creek Trail trailhead, located behind the shelter/restroom adjoining the parking area. The trailhead for the Overlook Trail is about 15 yards to the right. This is where the hike will end. The trail heads slightly up and into the woods and is blazed with white blazes painted on trees.

Pass a path on the left that leads down the hill to a bed-and-breakfast. A sign on the right states OLD TRACE SEGMENT. This portion is one of the few sections of the Old Natchez Trace in Tennessee that accommodates hikers. Take time to imagine the travelers of 200 years ago who followed this road and faced not only the natural hazards but bandits and hostile Indians too. Do not investigate the area off the trail. Copperheads and rattlesnakes, which are both venomous snakes, and black widow and brown recluse spiders call this home.

At 0.7 mile, pass the remnants of a wire fence. In 100 yards reach a T and take the right branch, heading north, causing the trail to double back. This leads to the Overlook Trail and the overlook, which is 0.25 mile away. The left branch continues the Garrison Creek Trail to the Old Trace trailhead and parking area. In a short distance the white blazes will be replaced by blue blazes, identifying the Overlook Trail.

In fall, small butterflies can be seen gathering around puddles here. Bear hard left, heading south to reach the overlook, which is bordered by a four-rail split-rail fence. A sweeping view of the Garrison Creek valley can be seen from the left side of the overlook. Continue on the trail by using the opening on the right side of the fence. The trail is flat for a short distance, then slopes sharply down and then flattens.

Bear hard left as the trail doubles back on itself. There is a gully that separates the south and northeast sections of the trail. A seasonal creek can be seen at the bottom of the gully. Bear left and cross a short bridge over the creek. Turn right at the end of the bridge. Notice the clumps of vines, including wild grape, climbing up the trees. Follow the trail as it heads due north until reaching a split-rail fence. This is the trailhead for the Overlook Trail and ends the hike.

Miles and Directions

0.0 Start at the Garrison Creek Trail trailhead, behind the shelter, at the south side of the parking area. Head south and slightly up. The Garrison Creek Trail is identified with white blazes painted on trees.

0.2 Continue following the white blazes as the trail completes a semicircle, still heading south.

0.3 Pass a path on the left that leads down the hill to a bread-and-breakfast. A sign on the right identifies this as OLD TRACE SEGMENT. Continue following the trail south through the woods.

0.5 The trail continues south. There is a 25-foot drop-off along the right edge of the trail; use caution. A few limestone slabs temporarily form the trail surface, requiring some stepping up and down.

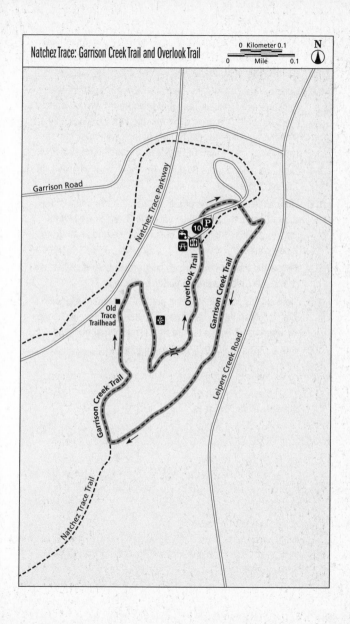

Natchez Trace: Garrison Creek Trail and Overlook Trail

0   Kilometer 0.1

0   Mile   0.1

N

Garrison Road

Natchez Trace Parkway

10 P

Overlook Trail

Old
Trace
Trailhead

Garrison Creek Trail

Garrison Creek Trail

Leipers Creek Road

Natchez Trace Trail

0.7 Follow the white blazes as the trail heads up and then flattens, still heading south. Pass the remnants of a wire fence. Bear slightly right, to the west.

0.8 Reach a T; take the right branch, which in 0.25 mile becomes the Overlook Trail, and head north. White blazes mark the trail for a short distance—then the Overlook Trail is identified by blue blazes. The left branch continues the Garrison Creek Trail to the Old Trace trailhead and parking area.

1.0 Continue following the Overlook Trail north as it weaves through the woods.

1.1 The trail is near the top of the ridge as it bears south to the right to reach the overlook. Leave the Overlook Trail by taking the opening through the split-rail fence and head down, going south.

1.3 Follow the trail as it continues south, then bear hard left as the trail doubles back and heads northeast.

1.4 Bear slightly left, still heading north. A seasonal creek bed is on the left about 15 feet away. The trail is narrow and edged by weeds as it heads toward the Overlook Trail trailhead.

1.6 End the hike at the Overlook Trail trailhead.

11 Mill Creek Greenway Trail

This in-city hike is especially convenient for the folks in Antioch. It takes you around Antioch Middle School, the community center, and then along Mill Creek. The shallow, nearly pristine creek and woods bordering it provide good habitat for wildlife in this residential area. There are plans to lengthen the Mill Creek Greenway Trail by continuing it to Ezell Park and adding a loop to it. Contact the Antioch Parks and Recreation Department for more information.

Start: Mill Creek Greenway Trail trailhead, adjacent to the Antioch Community Center parking area
Distance: 3.0-mile out-and-back
Approximate hiking time: 1.5 hours
Difficulty: Easy
Trail surface: Asphalt
Best season: Year-round
Other trail users: Bicyclists, strollers, wheelchairs, joggers, dog walkers
Canine compatibility: Leashed dogs permitted

Fees and permits: None required
Schedule: Dawn to dusk
Maps: USGS: Antioch; large map board at the trailhead
Trail contact: Antioch Parks and Recreation, 1523 New Hall Rd., Antioch 37013; (615) 315-9363; www.greenwaysfor nashville.org
Other: Water and restrooms available in the Antioch Community Center; portable toilet at the parking area

Finding the trailhead: From the west side of Nashville, take I-40 East via the ramp on the left and go 4 miles toward Knoxville. Keep right to take I-24 East, via exit 213A, toward Chattanooga and go 5.7 miles. Take the East Haywood Lane exit (exit 57B) toward Antioch and go 0.2 mile. Merge onto Haywood Lane and go 0.3 mile, then turn right onto Antioch Pike and go 1 mile. Turn right onto Blue Hole Road and go 0.2 mile to 5023 Blue Hole Rd., Antioch, on the right. *DeLorme Tennessee Atlas & Gazetteer:* Page 53 D4. GPS: N36 03.26 / W86 40.24

The Hike

A large map board at the trailhead lists various checkpoints along the trail. Several long benches are built into a fence on the outgoing right side of the trail, providing plenty of opportunities to kick back.

Head south from the trailhead, away from the community center and toward Antioch Middle School. Pass around the south end of the school, with the buildings on the left, separated from the trail by a chain-link fence. The trail slopes slightly down toward Mill Creek, heading northeast. A sitting area built in as part of a fence is on the right. The fence, which is about 40 feet long, discourages folks from going down to the creek. There is a sharp drop down to the creek behind the fence.

Pass the Antioch Middle School football field and bleachers on the left. In a short distance you come to a dirt path on the right that leads to a creek overlook. Take a short out and back to see the creek, whose clear water appears pristine and has a slight bluish tinge. Railroad tracks can be seen on the other side of the creek. Return to the trail and turn right, heading north.

The creek becomes hidden by shrubs and undergrowth as the trail slopes slightly down. Bear left, heading west; a bridge can be seen straight ahead. As you reach the underpass for the bridge, the creek is very close on the right. This is the best spot to look for animal tracks and small creek-loving creatures. Raccoons, opossums, deer, squirrels, and other animals come to the water. Return to the trail and cross under the bridge to the trail on the opposite side.

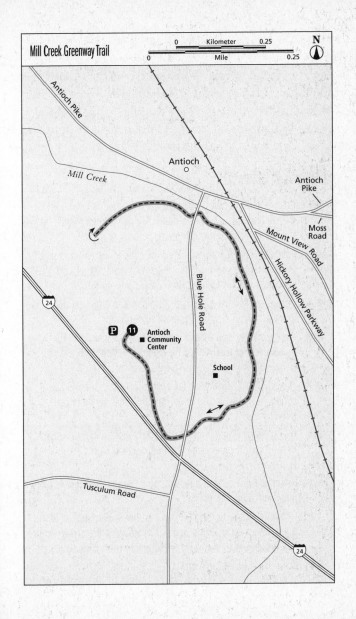

Mill Creek Greenway Trail

Kilometer
0   0.25

Mile
0   0.25

N

Antioch Pike

Mill Creek

Antioch ○

Antioch Pike

Moss Road

Mount View Road

Hickory Hollow Parkway

24

Blue Hole Road

P 11 Antioch Community Center

School

Tusculum Road

24

The right and left edges of the trail are mowed for a distance of 4 feet and are met by shrubs and a few trees. Birds, including robins in the spring, may be seen flying and foraging on the ground. Reach a T and take the right branch, with the creek on the right. Pass a path on the right that leads down to the creek. This is a good place to turn around and backtrack to the trailhead.

Miles and Directions

0.0 Start at the trailhead, adjacent to the Antioch Community Center parking area. Head south toward Antioch Middle School and turn left (northeast).

0.1 Follow the paved trail between the middle school on the left and residences on the right, then bear hard left around the school. Continue following the paved trail north.

0.4 Pass a rail fence on the right that has a sitting area built onto it. Continue following the trail north.

0.5 Pass a sitting area that creates a fence on the right. The middle school football field is behind the fence on the left. Continue following the trail north.

0.7 Take a short dirt path on the right that leads to a Mill Creek overlook. Return to the main trail and bear slightly right, heading north.

0.9 Follow the trail as it slopes down and goes under a bridge. Bear left at the end of the bridge, heading west. The creek is on the right.

1.1 Reach a T and take the right branch, heading northwest and following along the creek.

1.5 Continue following the trail in a northwesterly direction along the creek. A path on the right leads down to the creek. This is a good spot to stop and backtrack to the trailhead.

3.0 Arrive back at the trailhead.

12 Bledsoe Creek State Park: Loop and Shoreline Trails

Combine portions of the Loop and Shoreline Trails to see the best of Bledsoe Creek State Park. Small meandering streams border portions of the trail. Covered bridges and a gazebo add interest to the hike. This is the hike to see dozens of deer during spring and fall. Gallatin is 25 miles northeast of Nashville.

Start: Loop Trail trailhead, across the park road from the park headquarters

Distance: 2.8-mile lollipop

Approximate hiking time: 2.5 hours

Difficulty: Moderate

Trail surface: Bark mulch, dirt, and asphalt

Best season: Year-round

Other trail users: Dog walkers, joggers, and maybe wheelchairs and strollers on paved sections

Canine compatibility: Leashed dogs permitted

Fees and permits: None required

Schedule: Dawn to sunset

Maps: USGS: Hunters Point; maps available at the trailhead and at www.state.tn.us /environment/parks

Trail contacts: Park Manager, Bledsoe Creek State Park, 400 Zieglers Fort Rd., Gallatin 37066; (615) 452-3706; www.state.tn .us/environment/parks

Other: Water and restroom available in the park headquarters and in the campground

Finding the trailhead: Travel north from Nashville on I-65 and take exit 95 to Vietnam Veterans Boulevard. This will be TN 386. Take TN 386 to TN 31E North all the way into Gallatin. Pick up TN 25 East and travel approximately 7 miles to mile marker 20. Turn right onto Zieglers Fort Road. Travel 1 mile to the park entrance. *DeLorme*

The Hike

The Loop and Shoreline Trails have been combined so hikers can see the best of the 164-acre Bledsoe Creek State Park. The park covers much of the west shore of the Bledsoe Creek embayment of Old Hickory Lake. The section of the creek that has been impounded forms a small recreational lake.

The Loop Trail trailhead is picturesque with a small pond and a replica of a dug water well. Immediately go into dense woods following the trail, which is marked with red blazes. Cross a covered bridge, a unique feature of this park, over an unnamed creek. Within 100 feet, cross another covered bridge as the creek crosses the trail and meanders away.

Pass a trail marker post at about 0.7 mile, where the blue-blazed trail intersects the red-blazed trail, and turn right onto the blue-blazed trail. Pass a portion of the campground barely seen through the trees on the left. The trail breaks out into a clearing and then at about 1.0 mile reaches a park road. Carefully cross the road and adjoining parking area to reach the Shoreline Trail.

Reach a covered kiosk built by Eagle Scouts from BSA Troop 75 that contains a trail map. The left side of the trail parallels the impounded creek. At about 1.5 miles pass an opening on the left that allows for an investigation of the water. There are some limestone rocks near the trail and at the water's edge.

Continue past a chain-link fence on the right, which secures the park maintenance building. A path on the right leads to the park store. This may be a good spot to stop for some refreshments. Continue on the trail as it passes a small dock and boat launch area on the left. At 2.4 miles into the trail, pass a SHORELINE TRAIL sign on the right. Make a hard left and immediately cross a bridge over Bledsoe Creek.

Pass a small playground on the right. Reach another section of the park road and turn left, making a short out-and-back to the wildlife-viewing platform. You may see turtles in the water. Return to the trail, which is now the park road, and pass a gazebo on the right. Follow the road as it goes into the woods and becomes Birdsong Trail. This short paved loop is wheelchair and stroller accessible. Follow the Birdsong Trail for a short distance as it leads to the park headquarters. End the hike at the park headquarters, across the road from the trailhead.

Miles and Directions

0.0 Start at the Loop Trail trailhead, across the park road from the park headquarters. Head north. The Loop Trail is identified by red blazes.

0.2 Bear right at a large oak tree on the right. Pass a path that comes in from the left. Continue following the trail, bearing right.

0.3 Bear left and then right as the trail zigzags and begins to flatten. Bear right and cross a wooden covered bridge. Almost immediately cross another covered bridge.

0.5 Pass a red trail blaze and follow the trail down a sharp slope, then up a slight uphill grade, heading south by southeast.

0.7 Reach a trail marker post where the blue-blazed trail intersects the red-blazed trail. Turn right onto the blue-blazed trail and head west.

0.8 Pass a portion of the campground area and bear hard left, heading south.

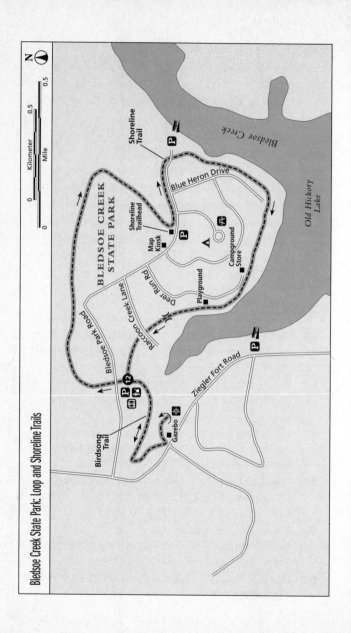

Bledsoe Creek State Park: Loop and Shoreline Trails

N

0   Kilometer   0.5
0   Mile   0.5

BLEDSOE CREEK STATE PARK

Birdsong Trail

P 12

Bledsoe Park Road

Raccoon Creek Lane

Deer Run Rd

Map Kiosk

Playground

Shoreline Trailhead

P

Shoreline Trail

P

Blue Heron Drive

Campground Store

Gazebo

Ziegler Fort Road

Bledsoe Creek

Old Hickory Lake

1.0 Reach a T intersection with the park road. Turn left and walk along the edge of the road. Use caution. Follow along the road until it reaches a large paved parking area, boat docks, and the Shoreline Trail trailhead.

1.2 Enter the Shoreline Trail with the woods on the right and the Bledsoe Creek impoundment on the left. Pass Rabbit Jump campsites 23 to 35, a small playground, picnic tables, grills, and a water spigot to the right. Continue heading south.

1.5 Continue following the red-blazed trail, with the impoundment on the left. Pass a clearing on the left that leads to the water's edge. Investigate the pond life and return to the trail, heading southwest.

1.6 The campground is on the right, about 150 feet away, through the trees. Continue following the trail as it snakes between the impoundment on the immediate left and campground on the right.

1.8 Follow the red-blazed trail past campsites 53 and 54 on the right. Bear right, away from the impoundment, heading northwest.

2.0 Pass a fenced area on the right that surrounds the park maintenance building. The park store is adjacent to the maintenance area. A path leads to the park store. Continue following the trail north.

2.2 The trail follows the creek's edge, heading north. There is a 25-foot clearing, allowing access to the edge of the impoundment. The campgrounds are to the right but are not visible.

2.3 Pass a SHORELINE TRAIL sign on the right, next to a clearing containing a playground area. Cross the playground area to the SHORELINE TRAIL sign on the opposite side and continue following Shoreline Trail, heading north.

2.4 Follow the trail until it makes a hard right, still heading north, and cross a wood bridge over Bledsoe Creek. The tail end of the impoundment is to the left. Turn right at the end of the bridge. Pass a gazebo along the park road and go left to reach a wildlife-viewing platform over the creek.

2.5 Return to the trail and pass a gazebo. Follow the paved trail into the woods, where it becomes Birdsong Trail. Birdsong Trail accommodates strollers and wheelchairs.

2.7 Reach a T and take the right branch, heading north, and follow it to the park headquarters.

2.8 End the hike at the park headquarters, across the road from the trailhead.

13 Cedars of Lebanon State Park: Cedar Glade Interpretive Trail

This is an excellent hike for families with young children or folks who are curious about cedar glades. Illustrated information signs along the edge of the trail explain the various features and creatures of a cedar glade. Cedars of Lebanon is 27 miles northeast of Nashville.

Start: Cedar Glade Interpretive Trail trailhead, adjacent to the headquarters parking area

Distance: 0.6-mile counterclockwise loop

Approximate hiking time: 1 hour, to allow time to read information signs

Difficulty: Easy

Trail surface: Bark mulch, dirt, some asphalt

Best season: Year-round

Other trail users: Dog walkers

Canine compatibility: Leashed dogs permitted

Fees and permits: None required

Schedule: 8:00 a.m. to 10:00 p.m.

Maps: USGS: Vine; trail maps and interpretive brochures available at the park headquarters

Trail contact: Park Manager, Cedars of Lebanon State Park, 328 Cedar Forest Rd., Lebanon 37090; (615) 443-2769; www .state.tn.us/environment/parks

Other: Water and restrooms are available at the park headquarters and picnic area. There is no potable water or restrooms on the trail. Take adequate water, use insect repellent, and wear a hat.

Finding the trailhead: From the south side of Nashville, take I-40 East via the ramp on the left toward Knoxville for 20 miles. Take US 231 South, exit 238, toward Lebanon/Hartsville and go 0.1 mile. Turn right onto US 231/South Cumberland Street/TN 10

and continue to follow US 231/TN 10 for 6.4 miles. Turn left on Cedar Forest Road, go 0.3 mile to 328 Cedar Forest Rd., Lebanon, and proceed to the park headquarters. *DeLorme Tennessee Atlas & Gazetteer:* Page 54 D2. GPS: N36 05.51 / W86 19.88

The Hike

The Cedar Glade Interpretive Trail is located in the 900-acre Cedars of Lebanon State Park, in the heart of the middle Tennessee karst area, which includes cedar glades. Less than 100 square miles of functional cedar glade remain in the country. The trail has a number of information signs that describe the features of a cedar glade.

From the trailhead adjacent to the parking area at the park headquarters, head west and almost immediately reach a covered kiosk. Turn right at the kiosk, temporarily heading north, then bear left until heading south. Head slightly downhill into the woods, which have some hardwoods but are predominantly cedar. Look for small clumps of reindeer moss, growing in circular clumps 12 to 15 inches in diameter and 8 to 12 inches high. Bear hard left at the interpretive sign and head slightly down.

Pass the second interpretive sign, which describes some geological features of the cedar glade. Almost immediately cross a short bridge over a seasonal creek and bear slightly to the right. With all this weaving right and left, the trail leads generally south. Pass another interpretive sign that lists some plants common to glades. In the spring look for butterflies, including yellow and white sulphurs, viceroys, and tiger swallowtails. They like to congregate around small puddles of water. Look into the woods and try to identify some of the trees, which include the winged elm, with its gray bark with shallow fissures and its small, toothed leafs.

The redbud is also in these woods, recognized by its heart-shaped leaves and in the fall by its bean-pod-like fruit that is 2 to 3 inches long.

Reach a sinkhole that is 5 feet from the left side of the trail. The hole is about 90 feet long and 25 feet wide. Use caution when going past these holes. Continue heading generally east and then nearly double back as the trail follows obliquely northwest. Listen for the raucous cry of the blue jay. This medium-size bird often tries to bully other birds. The call *pic-a-tuk* identifies the summer tanager, and its solid rosy red color makes it easy to spot.

Continue heading northwest and watch for small animals, including frogs, salamanders, lizards, and rabbits. Take the time to inspect the rotting tree stumps that adjoin the trail, looking for insects, lichen, and fungus. Pass an information sign, which honors Dr. Elsie Quarterman and her work in preserving the cedar glades, before reaching the trailhead and ending the hike.

Miles and Directions

0.0   Start at the Cedar Glade Interpretive Trail trailhead, at the edge of the parking area by the park headquarters and head west.

0.1   Turn right at the kiosk near the trailhead and within 100 yards bear left and then hard right, passing an interpretive sign. Bear hard left at the sign. The trail weaves a little as it leads to the next interpretive sign.

0.2   Continue following the asphalt trail, bearing left and crossing over a rustic bridge.

0.3   Pass an interpretive sign on the left and bear right, heading east from the sign. Pass a large sinkhole about 5 feet off the trail, bearing left around the edge.

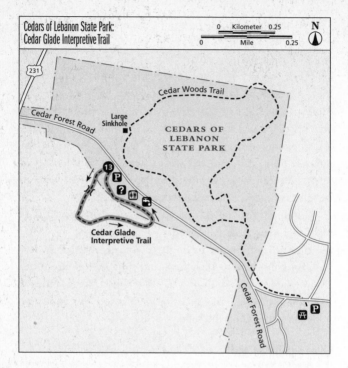

Cedars of Lebanon State Park:
Cedar Glade Interpretive Trail

Kilometer 0.25
Mile 0.25
N

Cedar Woods Trail

231

Cedar Forest Road

Large Sinkhole

CEDARS OF LEBANON STATE PARK

13 P

?

Cedar Glade Interpretive Trail

Cedar Forest Road

0.4 Follow the trail generally heading east. Make a hard left and reach an interpretive sign. The trail weaves a bit and passes two more interpretive signs.

0.5 The trail leads straight ahead and up a minor slope. Pass another interpretive sign and bear left, then immediately right. Continue following the trail as it heads northwest. Bear left and then right until reaching an interpretive sign. Follow the trail going north, toward the trailhead.

0.6 Arrive back at the trailhead.

14 Percy Priest Lake: Three Hickories Trail

This is an excellent hike for families with young children. The interpretive brochure explains many sites on the trail that take you through the woods and karst topography, with its limestone outcrops and sinkholes. Watch for turtles and waterbirds along the shoreline of the lake.

Start: Three Hickories Trail trailhead, adjacent to the parking area
Distance: 1.3-mile counterclockwise loop
Approximate hiking time: 1 hour
Difficulty: Easy
Trail surface: Dirt, rock
Best season: Year-round
Other trail users: Dog walkers
Canine compatibility: Leashed dogs permitted
Fees and permits: None required

Schedule: Dawn to 8:00 p.m. (gates locked at 8:00 p.m.)
Maps: USGS: Hermitage; trail maps and interpretive guides available at the park headquarters
Trail contact: U.S. Army Corps of Engineers, 3737 Bell Rd., Nashville 37214-2660; (615) 889-1975; www.recreation.gov
Other: Bicycles are not allowed on the trail. Water fountains and restrooms are available in the campground adjoining the parking area.

Finding the trailhead: From downtown Nashville take I-40 East 7 miles to exit 221B. Turn right on Old Hickory Boulevard and then left on Bell Road (there are Corps directional signs from this point on). Turn right on New Hope Road and go 1 mile, then turn right on Stewarts Ferry Pike and left on Old Hickory Boulevard for 1 mile to the Cook Recreation Area. The parking area is adjacent to the lake and campground area. The trail entrance is across from the amphitheater

in the day-use area. *DeLorme Tennessee Atlas & Gazetteer:* Page 53
D7. GPS: N36 08.15 / W86 36.12

The Hike

This is karst and cedar glade country. A karst is an area with
little to no topsoil, with limestone outcrops reaching to the
surface. The underlayer of limestone is gradually dissolved
by water seeping through, allowing caves, passageways, and
underground streams to be formed. Over time the top layers of limestone over the caves collapse, forming sinkholes
and crevasses, which are the signature features of a karst.
Cedar glades are also associated with karst areas. The glades
are thick stands of usually red cedar trees that surround a
limestone-surfaced, gravel-strewn meadow.

Before your hike, stop at the ranger post located at the
entrance and ask for a trail map and interpretive guide.
Drive to the large paved parking area adjacent to the lake.
From the trailhead, go immediately into the cedar woods,
following a short connector trail to a Y, where the loop
starts. Take the right branch and follow in a counterclockwise direction to keep the interpretive stations in sequence.
(One loop was chosen for this hike among the several on
the trail; therefore, you will not see all the interpretive stations on this hike. Use the trail map to locate the other
loops.)

Follow the loop south, passing Interpretive Station 2
on the left. Notice the large number of hickory trees in
the woods—the trail could have been named the Three
Hundred Hickories Trail! In the fall hundreds of hickory
nuts fall to the ground. Reach a fence surrounding a large
sinkhole and crevasse. You can see horizontal layers of limestone along the sides of the sinkhole. The Shawnee called

these *beinshawee,* meaning "deep water." A few locals have adopted this term, but pronounce it *boomshaw.*

You can see the lake through the trees on the right, about 300 feet away. Take a hard left and temporarily head away from the lake. The trail then bears back toward the lake while passing Interpretive Station 6. This is an easy spot to take a short out-and-back to the lakeshore. Look around for animal and bird tracks. Return to the trail and head north and then west, bearing away from the lake.

Pass Interpretive Station 8 on the right and bear hard right. Reach a Y and take the left branch. Pass a blue blaze and take a hard left, heading west to end the hike at the trailhead.

Miles and Directions

0.0 Start at the Three Hickories Trail trailhead at the edge of the paved parking area. Head east, passing Interpretive Station 1 at the trailhead. The trail is identified with blue blazes on trees.

0.1 Within 100 feet of the trailhead, reach a Y and take the right branch, heading southeast, then bear right, heading south (this will keep the trail signs relating to the interpretive guide in sequence). Pass Interpretive Station 2.

0.2 Continue following the trail around a fence protecting a large sinkhole and bear left, heading southeast. Pass Interpretive Stations 3 and 4 and continue following the trail southeast.

0.4 Follow the trail as it leads toward a boundary fence, then follow along the fenceline, heading north. Bear left, going away from the fence, and pass Interpretive Station 5. Percy Priest Lake can be seen on the right. Bear hard left, heading west away from the lake, and then right toward the shore.

0.6 Make your own short out-and-back through the trees to the edge of the lake. Return to the trail and bear slightly

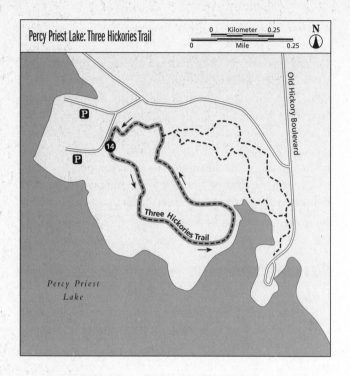

Percy Priest Lake: Three Hickories Trail

0 Kilometer 0.25
0   Mile   0.25

N

Old Hickory Boulevard

P

P

14

Three Hickories Trail

Percy Priest Lake

left. Continue heading west, away from the lake. Then bear northwest.

0.9 Continue following the trail northwest as it weaves around limestone outcrops and goes up and down minor slopes. This is the most strenuous section of the hike.

1.0 Reach a Y and take the left branch, heading west toward Interpretive Station 16 and the trailhead.

1.1 Pass Interpretive Station 16 on the right and bear hard left, heading west by northwest. The trail is straight and flat as it heads southwest toward the trailhead.

1.3 Arrive back at the trailhead

15 Long Hunter State Park: Couchville Lake Trail

Lake, woods, and tree lovers will appreciate the Couchville Lake Arboretum, which borders the trail. Wildlife lovers will like it too, as they may see deer and waterbirds here. A 300-foot wooden bridge crosses the lake and affords great photo ops. Many short out-and-back paths lead to the lake's edge and several ponds that border the trail.

Start: Couchville Lake Trailhead, adjacent to the boathouse
Distance: 2.1-mile clockwise loop
Approximate hiking time: 1.5 hours
Difficulty: Easy
Trail surface: Asphalt
Best season: Year-round
Other trail users: Birders, wheelchairs, strollers
Canine compatibility: Dogs not permitted

Fees and permits: None required
Schedule: 7:00 a.m. to sunset
Maps: USGS: LaVergne; trail maps and interpretive guides available at park office
Trail contact: Long Hunter State Park, 2910 Hobson Pike, Hermitage 37076; (615) 885-2422; www.state.tn.us/environment /parks
Other: Water and restrooms available at the park office and boathouse

Finding the trailhead: From the east side of Nashville, take I-40 East to Mount Juliet Road, exit 226A. Go south (right) 6.2 miles to the main park entrance and proceed to the headquarters. *DeLorme Tennessee Atlas & Gazetteer:* Page 53 D7. GPS: N36 05.67 / W86 32.66

The Hike

Couchville Lake was formed in 1968 when Percy Priest Lake was created. The Couchville Lake Arboretum that borders the trail was the first certified arboretum in a Tennessee state park. This 2,800-acre park with more than 17 miles of trails, ranging from less than a mile to 6.0 miles, may offer hikers the best combination of hikes near Nashville.

Pick up a trail map and interpretive brochure at the park headquarters and drive the short distance to the boathouse parking area. The hike starts at the Couchville Lake Trail trailhead adjacent to the boathouse. Hiking in the late afternoon affords the opportunity to see the sun set across the lake, an inspiring sight.

Pass the first of several concrete or gravel paths that lead to fishing platforms. Leaf patterns painted on the trail surface relate to the *Arboretum Interpretive Guide,* which describes the trees.

Keep alert for wild animals, especially deer feeding in the woods. Early morning and late afternoon afford the best opportunities for viewing. Reach a gravel path that leads to the lake and take the opportunity to go to the edge and investigate the water world. Continue following the loop as the lake comes in and out of view. Even though the trail is shown as a near-perfect loop on the map, it zigs and zags, so at any time the hike could go in an opposite direction for a short distance.

Follow the trail as it bears right to a 300-foot bridge that crosses the north part of the lake. After crossing the bridge, make a hard right. Pass a small seasonal pond on the left and look for animal tracks leading to the pond.

At about 1.0 mile you reach a small A-frame shelter. The shelter has benches and is a good place to sit and look around for a few minutes. Make a hard right after the shelter and break into a patch of open canopy. Watch for limestone outcrops and one section that is flat and resembles a sidewalk.

Continue straight and then take a hard right around the end of the lake. Pass two small seasonal ponds on the left, with a path leading to them. Look for a limestone "wall" over 4 feet high about 20 feet away. At the end of the wall, bear hard right and then left past a bench. Pass the arboretum signs for CHINQUAPIN OAK and VIRGINIA CREEPER to end the hike.

Miles and Directions

0.0   Start at the Couchville Lake Trail trailhead, across the parking area at the boathouse.

0.2   Follow the trail, passing several arboretum information signs. Pass a gravel path to the right that leads to the lake.

0.3   Pass a wood bench overlooking the lake. From the bench bear left, then right, continuing in a northwest direction. Arrive at another bench and take a hard right.

0.5   Follow the trail as it weaves right and left between the trees, with the lake on the right. Continue to pass arboretum information signs. Reach and cross the 300-foot bridge that spans the lake. Bear hard right at the end of the bridge and follow the trail southeast.

0.7   Pass a bench and follow the trail along the lake edge while passing arboretum information signs. The lake is on the right, about 45 feet away.

0.8   Follow the trail as it bends left and right between the trees. Pass a bench and bear slightly left. After passing some arboretum information signs, bear hard right. This leg of the loop heads in a southeasterly direction.

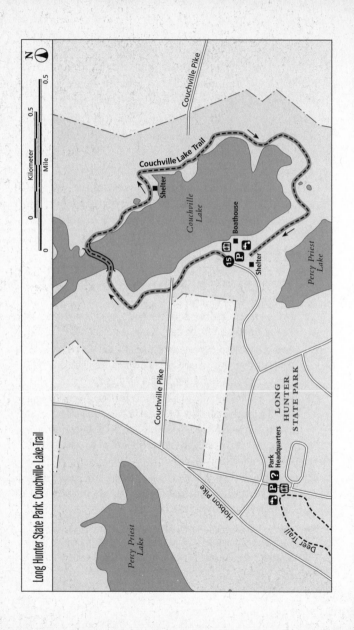

Long Hunter State Park: Couchville Lake Trail

Couchville Lake Trail

Couchville Lake

Percy Priest Lake

Percy Priest Lake

Couchville Pike

Couchville Pike

Hobson Pike

Shelter

Shelter

Boathouse

Park Headquarters

LONG HUNTER STATE PARK

Deer Trail

N

Kilometer
0   0.5
0   0.5
Mile

0.9   Pass a seasonal pond on the left. The lake is on the right, about 15 feet away. Continue following the trail along the lake edge.

1.0   Reach a small A-frame shelter that has benches. After visiting the shelter, return to the trail. Follow the trail a short distance and make a hard right, then head southwest across the south end of the lake.

1.2   Continue to follow the trail past a bench and arboretum information signs. The trail zigzags as it generally follows the lake edge to the right. Pass a gravel path to a fishing pier about 35 feet to the right. The trail bears slightly to the left and then weaves right and left, generally following the lake edge in a northwesterly direction.

1.5   Pass several arboretum information signs and a bench as the trail tracks right and left. Follow the trail, with the lake on the right.

1.8   A path on the right leads to the lake; take a short out-and-back to investigate the shoreline. Pass two small seasonal ponds on the left and a concrete sidewalk on the right that leads to a fishing pier. Look for a limestone wall, about 4 feet high.

2.1   Arrive back at the trailhead.

16 Henry Horton State Park: Wild Turkey Trail

This is a hike for those who love woods, ponds, and the opportunity to see wildlife, including wild turkeys. Hickory and oak trees dominate the woods. A small pond is jumping with frogs and toads in the fall. Chapel Hill is 50 miles south of Nashville

Start: The trailhead adjacent to the parking area next to the park maintenance building.
Distance: 2.3-mile clockwise loop
Approximate hiking time: 1.5 hours
Difficulty: Easy
Trail surface: Dirt
Best season: Year-round
Other trail users: Dog walkers, joggers
Canine compatibility: Leashed dogs permitted
Fees and permits: None required

Schedule: 8:00 a.m. to 10:00 p.m; winter hours 8:00 a.m. to sundown
Maps: USGS: Farmington; trail maps available at the park office
Trail contacts: Park Manager, Henry Horton State Park, 4209 Nashville Highway, Chapel Hill 37034; (931) 364-7724; www .state.tn.us/environment/parks
Other: Restrooms and water are available at the campground and park office. There is no potable water or restrooms on the trail.

Finding the trailhead: From the south side of Nashville, take I-40 East via the ramp on the left toward Knoxville and go 0.9 mile. Merge onto I-65 South, via exit 210, toward Huntsville and go 36.5 miles. Take US 412/TN 99, exit 46, toward Columbia and go 0.2 mile. Turn left onto US 412/Bear Creek Pike/TN 99. Continue to follow Bear Creek Pike/TN 99 for 4 miles. Then take a slight right onto US 431 and go 0.8 mile. Turn right onto TN 99 and go 7.4 miles. Turn right onto US 31A, go 0.8 mile, and pass the park entrance. Continue 1 mile past the park office to Warner Road and turn left. Follow Warner Road to the park maintenance building on the right. Trailhead is adjacent to the park maintenance parking area. *DeLorme Tennessee Atlas & Gazetteer:* Page 37 C6. GPS: N35 35.010 / W86 41.396.

The Hike

The Wild Turkey Trail is located in the 1,200-acre Henry Horton State Park, near Chapel Hill. Stop at the park headquarters to pick up a map, and then leave the park and turn left onto US 31A and go 1 mile to Warner Road and turn left. Follow Warner Road and turn right into the parking area by the park maintenance building. The trailhead is adjacent to the parking area. Go into the woods, heading southeast. Depending on the season of the year, mosquitoes can be a nuisance—especially spring and fall,

The trail bears right, heading southeast. Continue on the trail until it takes a hard left, heading east. In less than 0.1 mile make a hard right heading south. Follow the trail as it veers slightly left and reaches a seasonal pond about 50 feet to the right. Take the path to the edge of the pond, where there is a bench facing the water. This is one of the most interesting sections of the hike. In spring and fall the pond is overrun with frogs, toads, and other smaller amphibians. Near the edge of the pond is a good place to look for animal and bird tracks.

Return to the trail and cross over a small seasonal creek. Follow the trail southwest until it takes a hard right turn, heading west. The trail undulates up and down and veers right, left, and back right. In the fall look for acorns and hickory nuts scattered across the trail. Look for 1-inch-long acorns with a skinny cap. These identify the northern red oak, which thrives in Tennessee. This oak holds it leaves longer than most, and the 4-foot, 10-inch-long leaves turn red in autumn.

Follow the red blazes heading west until the trail makes an oblique right, heading northeast. Continue on the trail as it wanders back and forth for 0.5 mile, passing a bench on the right. A flock of wild turkeys have been seen in this area, but they wander around, roosting in trees at night. The trail bends left, heading north for a short distance, where it makes a hard right, heading east to the end of the trail. The trail ends at the opposite side of the parking area.

Miles and Directions

0.0 Start at the Wild Turkey Trail trailhead, adjacent to the park maintenance building parking area. Head southeast going clockwise. The trail is identified with red blazes.

0.1 Follow the trail into woods and past a few limestone out-crops in heavy woods.

0.4 Follow trail as it heads southeast, then east for less than 0.1 mile, and then south to reach a seasonal pond.

0.5 Head west from the seasonal pond for less than 0.1 mile.

0.6 Follow the trail as it turns hard left, heading south by south-west.

0.8 Pass a park maintenance road that crosses the trail.

0.9 Follow the trail southwest until it takes a hard left, heading west.

1.2 Bear oblique right and head northwest through woods and a few limestone outcrops.

1.7 Continue following the red blazes northeast and reach a bench on the right.

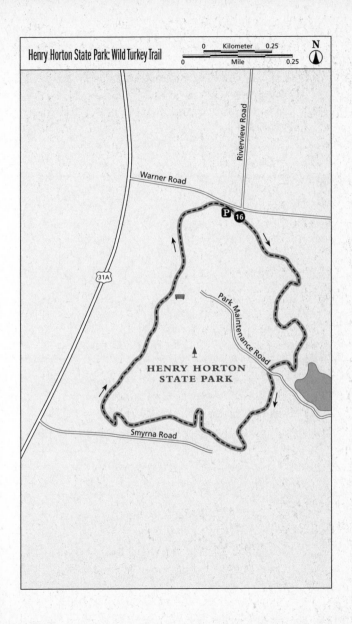

Henry Horton State Park: Wild Turkey Trail

Kilometer
0   0.25
Mile
0   0.25

N

Riverview Road

Warner Road

P 16

31A

Park Maintenance Road

HENRY HORTON
STATE PARK

Smyrna Road

1.8 Continue northeast and follow the trail as it turns left, heading due north.

1.9 The trail bears hard right, heading east toward the end of the trail.

2.3 End the hike at the opposite end of the parking area from the trailhead.

17 Duck River State Natural Area: Cheeks Bend Vista Trail

This is a hike for those who love woods, karst geography, and major rivers. Limestone outcroppings cross the trail. Follow the bluff along the river, which comes in and out of view and is 70 to 100 feet below the trail. Reach the overlook and enjoy the sweeping view.

Start: Cheeks Bend trailhead, on the west side of the small parking area off Cheeks Bend Road
Distance: 2.3-mile lollipop
Approximate hiking time: 1.5 hours
Difficulty: Easy
Trail surface: Dirt, limestone
Best season: Year-round
Other trail users: Dog walkers
Canine compatibility: Leashed dogs permitted

Fees and permits: None required
Schedule: Dawn to 1 hour before dusk
Maps: USGS: Glendale; trail maps not available
Trail contacts: Tennessee State Natural Areas; www.state.tn.us /environment/na/natareas/
Other: No potable water or restrooms on the trail

Finding the trailhead: From the south side of Nashville, merge onto I-40 East/I-65 South toward Knoxville/Huntsville and go 0.9 mile. Merge onto I-65 South, via exit 210, toward Huntsville and proceed 36 miles. Take US 412/TN 99 exit 46 toward Columbia/Chapel Hill and travel 0.2 mile. Turn left onto US 412/TN 99 and go 4 miles. Then take a slight right onto US 431/TN 99 and go 5.7 miles. Take a slight right onto Jordan Lane and go 0.4 mile, where Jordan Lane becomes Sowell Mill Pike. Go 2.9 miles on Sowell Mill Pike to Cheeks Bend Road. Turn right onto Cheeks Bend Road and go 1.5

miles to the parking area and trailhead. *DeLorme Tennessee Atlas & Gazetteer:* Page 37 D4. GPS: N35 34.088 / W86 53.094

The Hike

The Cheeks Bend Vista Trail is located in the Cheeks Bend State Natural Area, which is part of the 2,135-acre Duck River Natural Area Complex. From the trailhead, head west, into the woods. Bear left to reach a kiosk with a large trail map. Most of the trail is singletrack. Bear left, passing several small limestone slabs on the left. Follow the blue-blazed trail west as the trail features limestone outcrops and slabs, indicating this is karst territory ("karst" is a geographic feature).

Reach two large flat pieces of limestone on the left side of the trail. They are just high enough to sit on and rest a moment. The Duck River can occasionally be seen through the woods and down a slope on the left. Pass a trail on the left that is marked CLOSED. Orange tape is across the trail and a sign states BOUNDARY TWRA—SPECIAL REGULATIONS IN EFFECT.

This trail is interesting because it rarely goes straight and each turn can present some new view. Be alert, since the left side of the trail is edged by some 50-foot drop-offs. Pass a narrow crevasse on the left side that is 2 feet wide by 20 feet long and down 10 feet. Bear right, away from the crevasse, then slightly up. After bearing hard right, pass a trail that is marked CLOSED and has orange tape across it. This is the other end of the trail passed at about 0.5 mile. The trail now heads due north and forms a counterclockwise loop.

Continue following the trail as it bears left, heading west, and then left again, heading south. The river can be seen straight ahead and down about 80 feet. Make a hard left near the edge of the bluff, which completes the loop, and head east, with the river on your right. This is the most picturesque portion of the hike. Use caution, since the edge of the trail is sometimes only 10 feet from sheer drop-offs to the river, 80 feet below.

At about 1.0 mile reach the Duck River Overlook, which is positioned on solid limestone. Sweeping views of the river and surrounding countryside are great. Then investigate the sinkholes and crevasse to the left and to the rear. This is a good spot to rest and admire nature's works before backtracking to the trailhead.

Miles and Directions

0.0 Start at the Cheeks Bend Vista Trail trailhead adjacent to the small gravel parking area on Cheeks Bend Road and head northwest. The trail is identified with blue blazes. Immediately reach a kiosk with a trail map.

0.3 Pass through a small clearing, then make a hard left and cross over what looks like a stream of small limestone rocks. Continue straight west, passing several blue-blazed trees.

0.4 Continue following the trail west until you reach a path on the left that leads to an overlook to view the river. Take this short out-and-back path to the overlook and return to the trail heading west.

0.5 Pass a trail on the left that is marked with orange tape and a sign stating the trail is CLOSED. There is also a sign that states BOUNDARY TWRA—SPECIAL REGULATIONS IN EFFECT. Continue west on the Cheeks Bend VistaTrail and then make a hard left, still heading west.

0.6 Pass a narrow crevasse on the left, about 20 feet long, and then bear right, away from the crevasse but still heading generally west, toward the river.

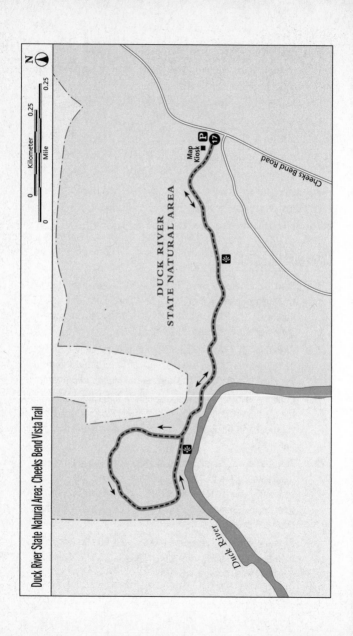

Duck River State Natural Area: Cheeks Bend Vista Trail

0.7 Bear hard left and pass a trail on the right that is posted as CLOSED. This is the other end of the trail you passed earlier. Continue heading generally north.

0.9 Reach a short path on the right, leading to the edge of the bluff with a good overlook of the river. Take this out and back and return to the trail, heading east.

1.0 Reach the Duck River Overlook. Use caution, as there are sheer drops of 70 to 100 feet. Investigate the typical karst sinkholes and limestone outcrops to the left. Backtrack to the trailhead.

2.3 Arrive back at the trailhead.

18 Murfreesboro Greenway: College Street Pond Loop

This is a great hike for folks who enjoy ponds and the creative use of a landfill, as well as for sun lovers. The loop leads to a pond with a small island that has formal gardens and a gazebo. Small waterfalls flow from the upper level to the lower level of the pond.

Start: Pond Loop Trail trailhead, adjacent to the parking area off College Street
Distance: 1.7-mile clockwise loop
Approximate hiking time: 1 hour
Difficulty: Easy
Trail surface: Asphalt
Best season: Sept–June
Other trail users: Joggers, in-line skaters, bicyclists, wheelchairs, strollers, dog walkers
Canine compatibility: Leashed dogs permitted
Fees and permits: None required

Schedule: Dawn to dusk
Maps: USGS Murfreesboro; large mounted trail map near each trailhead
Trail contact: Murfreesboro Greenway System, 697 Barfield Crescent Rd., Murfreesboro 37128; (615) 890-5333; www .murfreesborotn.gov
Other: There are restrooms at the reception center, but the center is not open every day. There is no potable water or restrooms on the trail.

Finding the trailhead: From the east side of Nashville, take I-40 East via the ramp on the left toward Knoxville and go 4 miles. Keep right to take I-24 East, exit 213A, toward Chattanooga and go 23.3 miles. Merge onto TN 840 East via exit 74B toward Lebanon and go 1.9 miles. Merge onto Northwest Broad Street via exit 55A toward

Murfreesboro and go 2.7 miles. Turn right onto Thompson Lane and go 0.3 mile, then turn left onto Old Nashville Highway and go 0.1 mile. Turn right onto West College Street and go 0.3 mile to 1902 West College St., in Murfreesboro. Proceed to the parking area and trailhead. *DeLorme Tennessee Atlas & Gazetteer:* Page 38 A2. GPS: N35 52.14 / W86 25.26

The Hike

Murfreesboro has created a boon for hikers by connecting trails and routing them along river and creek floodplains that normally would be considered unusable. A kiosk with a large color-coded map is located at the trailhead. Use caution crossing West College Street, and make a hard left onto the paved trail. Continue heading south until you come to a Y; take the left branch. Pass a bench on the left, constructed from steel rods. These benches are a signature feature of the trail.

Turn right and go slightly up, past a large meadow on the right that covers a closed landfill. Stop at a park bench on the left and look toward the pond and island. Three fountains can be seen in the pond. The water, grassy meadow area, and a few trees make this area good habitat for numerous species of birds, including killdeer, robins, doves, and red-winged blackbirds.

Bear right, then left, as the trail heads slightly down. Reach a Y and take the right branch. In a short distance reach a Y that has formal flower plantings around it and two benches with a large map board between them. Take the right branch and head a bit north and then west. Turn left and cross a bridge onto the island, which contains a reception center, a gazebo, formal flower plantings, benches, and picnic tables. A stream crosses the island and forms two small waterfalls that tumble down into the pond. Cross over the bricked surface to the opposite side of the island and cross a steel bridge to pick up the trail. Turn right, heading northwest, with a grassy meadow on the left and the pond on the right.

Pass several benches on the right, facing the pond. This is the best location to view the three floating fountains. Notice the gushing water flowing from a pipe at the head of the pond. This is repurified water from the city's water and sewer department. A large flock of Canada geese frolic in the fresh water.

Follow the trail around the pond to a Y and take the right branch, heading east for a short distance and then north. Continue following the trail along the large meadow (the closed landfill) on the right and pass a fenced area that contains a gas burner used to burn methane escaping from the landfill. Almost immediately reach a Y and take the left branch to backtrack to the trailhead.

Miles and Directions

0.0 Start at the Pond Loop Trail trailhead, adjacent to the paved parking area off West College Street.

0.1 Follow the asphalt trail and within 100 feet reach the stop sign at West College Street. Cross the street, using caution, and follow the trail, making a hard left and heading southeast.

0.5 Continue following the trail in a southeasterly direction. A trail comes in from the right; turn right onto this trail, heading west.

0.6 Reach a Y at a lamppost on the left and take the right branch, still heading west. Continue following the trail west.

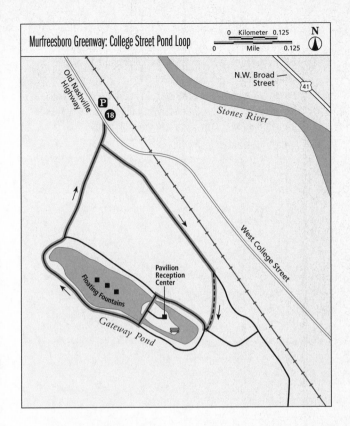

0.7 Pass a bench with a trail map board next to it. Reach a Y and take the right branch, heading temporarily north and then west. The island and pond are just ahead.

0.9 Follow the trail along the pond to the island, crossing one of two metal bridges. Cross the bridge on the west side of the island, reach a T, and take the right branch, still heading northwest. Follow the trail, with the pond on the right, as it makes a hard right, heading north.

1.3 Reach a Y and take the right branch, heading northeast. (The left branch is a sidewalk leading to a medical clinic.) Follow the trail as it bends around the north end of the pond.

1.4 Reach a Y and take the left branch, heading north. Continue following the trail a short distance until reaching a Y. Take the left branch and backtrack to the trailhead.

1.7 Arrive back at the trailhead.

19 Montgomery Bell State Park: Jim Bailey Nature Trail, Wildcat Trail, Ore Pit Trail, and Montgomery Bell Trail

This is a trail for those who love history, the woods, historic buildings, and creeks. Follow the trail up and down through woods past iron ore pits dug in 1801. Investigate the restored Presbyterian church complex from 1810. Burns is located 40 miles west of Nashville.

Start: Jim Bailey Nature Trail trailhead, adjacent to the park headquarters parking area

Distance: 4.8-mile counterclockwise loop

Approximate hiking time: 3 hours

Difficulty: More challenging

Trail surface: Dirt, asphalt

Best season: Year-round

Other trail users: Dog walkers, joggers

Canine compatibility: Leashed dogs permitted

Fees and permits: None required

Schedule: 8:00 a.m. to 10:00 p.m. (spring/summer), 8:00 a.m. to sundown (fall/winter)

Maps: USGS: Burns; trail maps available at the park headquarters

Trail contacts: Park Manager, Montgomery Bell State Park, P.O. Box 39, Burns 37029; www.state.tn.us/environment/parks

Other: Restrooms and water are available at the campground and park headquarters. There is no potable water or restrooms on the trail.

Finding the trailhead: From the west side of Nashville, merge onto I-40 West toward Memphis and travel 27 miles. Take TN 96, exit 182, toward Fairview/Dickson and proceed 0.1 mile; turn left onto TN 96 and go 10 miles. Take a slight right onto US 70 and go 3.6 miles. Turn right onto Jackson Hill Road and go less than 0.1 mile, where it becomes Bakers Work Road. Follow Bakers Work Road for less than 0.1 mile, where it becomes Jackson Hill Road. Follow Jackson Hill Road to 1020 Jackson Hill Rd. and turn right into the park. Follow the park road to the park headquarters. *DeLorme Tennessee Atlas & Gazetteer:* Page 52 D1. GPS: N36 6.082 / W87 17.070

The Hike

Stop at the park headquarters and pick up a map and interpretive brochures. This hike combines the Jim Bailey Nature Trail, the Wildcat Trail, the Ore Pit Trail, and the Montgomery Bell Trail to present the best of the 3,782-acre Montgomery Bell State Park. The hike covers several important areas in the park, including the Jim Bailey Nature Trail, the ore pits dug in the early 1800s for iron ore, the hardwood forests and creeks, and the restored 1810 Presbyterian church complex.

The Jim Bailey Nature Trail is the first area encountered. Follow the trail across a bridge over a meandering creek up the hill behind the park headquarters. The trail traverses back and forth across the hill, so sections of the trail just hiked can be seen. Follow the green blazes on small markers on trees. Reach the top of the hill, where the creek can be seen below. Cross two boardwalks across shallow gullies. Notice the large hardwood trees, including hickory and oak. Reach a T and take the right branch onto the Wildcat Trail, which is marked with blue blazes. The park office can be seen below and to the left.

Within 0.1 mile reach a Y and take the right branch, continuing on the Wildcat Trail. The left branch leads to the campground. Follow the trail along the top of the ridge and then head down. The trail zigzags as it works its way through the woods. Pass hardwood trees, including sugarberry. Reach the bottom and follow a small semicircle to a bridge over an unnamed creek. The creek has a small rapids that provides a good photo op. Follow the trail as it reaches a shelter and then bears left onto the Ore Pit Trail, which leads to the iron ore pits and is identified with blue blazes.

Bear left and pass several iron-ore pits that were dug around 1800 by laborers working for Montgomery Bell, for whom the park is named. Bell came from Pennsylvania seeking his fortune. He found iron ore, built several forges, and became one of the wealthiest men in Tennessee. Most of the area's trees were burned to create charcoal for the forges. Through careful management and work done by the Civilian Conservation Corps in the 1930s, today the area is forested and healthy.

The trail heads up and down as it follows the topography. Cross several shallow unnamed creeks. Break out into a clearing and the park road. Straight ahead is the Old Log House, which is a replica of the home of Reverend Samuel McAdow, who founded the Cumberland Presbyterian Church at this site in 1810. The area has sidewalks leading to a modern-day church and other historic buildings. This is about halfway through the hike. Cross over a bridge at the rear of the cabin. Reach a T and continue on the Ore Pit Trail.

Nearly 3.0 miles into the hike, reach a shelter and trail signs. Follow the trail to the left, along the side of the shelter. Continue through the woods, reach a park road, and pass the warehouse parking area. Continue following right around the warehouse until reaching a Y; take the left branch—the Montgomery Bell Trail. Continue following the trail until it reaches the parking area at the park headquarters.

Miles and Directions

0.0 Start at the Jim Bailey Trail trailhead, adjoining the parking area at the park headquarters. Head northwest. The trail is identified with green blazes.

0.1 Within 200 feet cross the bridge over the unnamed creek fed by Lake Acorn. Bear left, away from the creek, and head up the hill.

0.2 Reach the top of the hill and bear hard left, still heading northwest.

0.3 Cross a boardwalk and within 40 feet cross another boardwalk. Bear hard right and pass Jim Bailey Nature Trail marker 7.

0.5 Reach a T and take the right branch heading south onto the Wildcat Trail, which is identified with blue blazes. The left branch leads back to the park office.

0.6 Reach a Y and take the right branch staying on Wildcat Trail, heading northwest.

0.8 Cross a bridge over an unnamed shallow creek. Make a hard left at the end of the bridge, heading toward the Ore Pit Trail. Continue following blue blazes, heading south.

1.0 Head slightly down until reaching a shelter. Several trails meet at the shelter, creating a Y. Take the right branch, heading southwest onto the Ore Pit Trail, identified with red blazes.

1.3 Follow the Ore Pit Trail as it veers right and left around iron ore pits dug around 1800.

1.6 Continue to pass ore pits and earth mounds. The trail weaves back and forth but generally heads south. Use caution, since some trail sections on the right have sheer drop-offs. Continue following the red blazes.

1.9 Ford a shallow stream about 5 feet wide. Bear left, heading southeast until you reach a clearing.

2.0 Cross a park road and reach the historical Presbyterian church complex. Sidewalks lead to the restored cabin and church. Cross a bridge at the Old Log House and head slightly up on the Ore Pit and Montgomery Bell Trails.

2.5 Follow the red and white–blazed trail up and down the hills, through the woods. There are no significant landmarks. Reach a T and follow the left branch heading east and then sharply left, heading north.

2.8 Reach a shelter and follow the trail to the left of the shelter. Follow the red blazes as the trail follows a small semicircle.

3.0 Bear left at a red blaze, go slightly down, and reach a T. Take the right branch, heading east and following the red blazes.

3.2 Cross an asphalt park road. Reach a fenced area marked WAREHOUSE PARKING. There is a large sign giving distances to various locations. Follow the fence around the warehouse, heading northeast, then north, and then east.

3.6 Cross a long bridge over an unnamed shallow creek and immediately reach a Y. Take the left branch and follow the white-blazed Montgomery Bell Trail. A short section of the trail is very steep.

3.9 Follow the trail to the top of the ridge. Follow the white-blazed trail as it makes hard rights and lefts, still heading generally north.

4.0 Use caution in crossing an asphalt park road and follow the blue-blazed (Wildcat Trail) and white-blazed (Montgomery Bell Trail) trails.

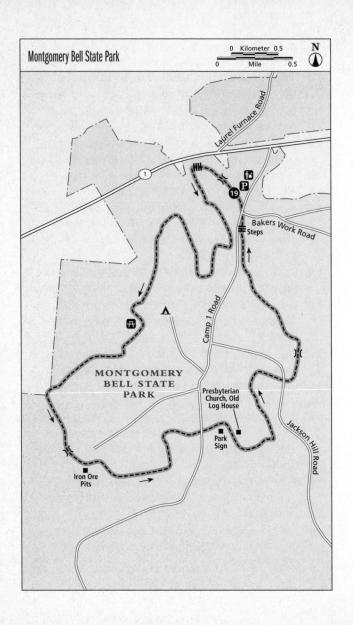

Montgomery Bell State Park

0   Kilometer   0.5

0   Mile   0.5

N

Laurel Furnace Road

1

Bakers Work Road

Steps

19

P

Camp 1 Road

MONTGOMERY
BELL STATE
PARK

Presbyterian
Church, Old
Log House

Park
Sign

Jackson Hill Road

Iron Ore
Pits

4.1 At the top of the ridge, reach a Y and take the left branch, heading north by northwest. Follow the white blazes as the trail veers right, left, and back right.

4.3 Pass a swampy area on the left and gully on the right.

4.5 Carefully go down thirty-four steps to where the terrain flattens.

4.6 Reach a Y and follow the left branch, which heads down toward the park office.

4.8 Arrive back at the trailhead.

20 Dunbar Cave State Natural Area: Lake Trail and Recovery Trail

This is a great hike for those who love nostalgia, woods, and lakes. Near the mouth of Dunbar Cave, go up the stairs to a concrete dance floor that in the late 1940s was filled with people dancing to the music of famous bands, including Tommy Dorsey's and Benny Goodman's.

Start: Recovery Trail trailhead, at the edge of the visitor center parking area
Distance: 2.4-mile clockwise loop
Approximate hiking time: 1.5 hours
Difficulty: Easy
Trail surface: Asphalt, dirt, mulch, concrete
Best season: Sept–June
Other trail users: Dog walkers, joggers
Canine compatibility: Leashed dogs permitted
Fees and permits: None required

Schedule: 8:00 a.m. to sunset
Maps: USGS: Clarksville; trail maps available at visitor center; large map boards along trail
Trail contact: Dunbar Cave State Natural Area, 401 Old Dunbar Rd., Clarksville 37043; (931) 648-5526; www.tnstateparks .com
Other: Water fountains and restrooms are available at the visitor center. There is no potable water or restrooms on the trail. Take adequate drinking water, use insect repellent and sunscreen, and wear a hat.

Finding the trailhead: From the north side of Nashville, take I-40 West toward Memphis and go 0.8 mile. Merge onto I-65 North via exit 208 toward I-24 West and go 2.1 miles. Merge onto I-24 West via exit 86A on the left toward Clarksville and go 2.2 miles. Keep left to take I-24 West via exit 88B toward Clarksville and go 36.6 miles.

Take TN 237 West, exit 8, and go 0.4 mile. Turn onto TN 237 and go 0.8 mile, then turn left onto Dunbar Cave Road and go 3 miles. Turn right onto Old Dunbar Cave Road and go 0.1 mile to 401 Old Dunbar Cave Rd. in Clarksville, then turn onto the park road and follow it to the visitor center and trailhead. *DeLorme Tennessee Atlas & Gazetteer:* Page 64 D1. GPS: N36 33.02 / W87 18.367

The Hike

This trail, combining the Recovery Trail and sections of the Lake Trail, is located in the 110-acre Dunbar Cave State Natural Area. Local lore has it that the cave was a favorite location for moonshiners during the 1920s.

Roy Acuff, an icon in country music, purchased Dunbar Cave in the 1940s. He used the site for entertainment shows featuring big bands like Benny Goodman's and Tommy Dorsey's. Big bands and dancing were the rage in the 1940s, and it was during this period that a large concrete structure, with three distinct arches, was poured in front of the cave entrance to serve as a dance floor. This striking structure is intact today, with the cave behind it and Swan Lake in front of it.

Head into the woods at the trailhead. Swan Lake is on the right. Reach a small map and a Y and take the left branch, heading north and still in the woods. There are a few cedar trees interspersed among the oak, beech, and sycamore trees. Reach a Y and take the left branch, following it to the right (northeast). Sections of the trail bear hard left and then hard right, temporarily heading in various directions for very short distances but then returning northeast.

Continue following the trail as it slopes up until reaching the top of the ridge. In a short distance bear hard right, heading south. In less than the length of a football field, make a hard right and head west. Turn right, heading west until reaching a boardwalk. Cross the boardwalk and make a hard left, heading south. Follow the trail up and down small slopes for less than 0.5 mile until reaching a T. Take the left branch, staying on the Recovery Trail and heading west. Continue following the trail until making a hard right as the trail doubles back on itself, then after a short distance cross a bridge over a gully. Start to bear right, heading north and then northwest, as the trail approaches Swan Lake.

Reach the edge of the lake, where there is a bench facing the water. Turn right at the bench onto the Lake Trail and head north. Continue following the trail along the water's edge and notice the many ducks that frequent the lake year-round. The large white concrete structure that used to house the dance floor is straight ahead. Go up the steps to explore the building, then return to the trail and follow it back to the visitor center and trailhead.

Miles and Directions

0.0   Start at the Recovery Trail trailhead, adjacent to the visitor center parking area and head north.

0.1   Pass picnic tables on the right and left. Woods are on both sides of the trail as it slopes up and down. Swan Lake is on the right but usually not visible.

0.2   Bear right, pass a guardrail, and reach a trail map and Y. Take the left branch, heading north. The right branch is a short leg to Dunbar Cave. Continue following the trail north, passing over some water bars made from 6-by-6 lumber.

0.3   Reach a Y and take the left branch, which is the Recovery Trail (the right branch is a short loop back to the trailhead). Continue following the trail as it bears hard right and heads northeast.

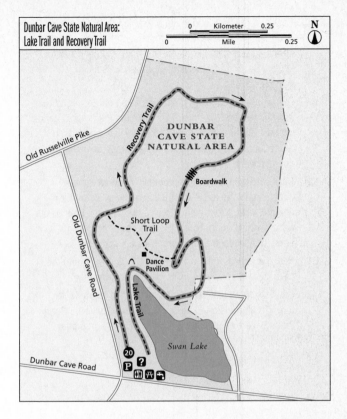

Dunbar Cave State Natural Area:
Lake Trail and Recovery Trail

0.5 Bear hard left, temporarily heading northwest, then bear right and pass a wood park bench on the right. Continue straight on the trail, through the hardwood trees, going northeast and slightly up. The trail flattens for a short distance, after which it weaves a bit and slopes up.

0.7 Reach the top of the ridge and make a hard right, heading east. Pass a park bench on the right. Continue bearing slightly to the right (east) as the trail slopes down. Bear hard right and follow the trail south. Continue following the trail as it makes a hard right and heads west.

1.0 Pass a park bench and make a hard left, heading south, and cross over a boardwalk. At the end of the boardwalk bear right and then left as the trail follows up and down slopes. Continue following the trail generally south, although it zigzags a little.

1.4 Follow the trail south as it undulates up and down and then has flat sections. Reach a T and take the left branch, heading east on the Recovery Trail (the right branch leads to the Short Loop Trail). Bear slightly left and then follow right, heading west.

1.7 Bear hard right, heading temporarily north as the trail doubles back on itself. The trail then bears left until it is heading west. Cross a short bridge over a gully. Start to bear right, heading north. Follow the trail down, bearing northwest through the woods as it approaches the lake.

2.0 Reach a bench at the lake's edge and turn right onto the Lake Trail, heading north. The trail borders the lake.

2.1 Continue north until reaching a large white concrete structure. Go up the steps to explore the dance pavilion. Return to the Lake Trail and follow it along the edge of the lake, heading south to the visitor center.

2.4 Arrive back at the trailhead.

Nashville Area Outdoor Clubs

Tennessee Trails Association
P.O. Box 41446
Nashville, TN 37204
1-888-445-3882
www.tennesseetrails.org

Tennessee Scenic Rivers Association
P.O. Box 159041
Nashville, TN 37215
www.paddleTSRA.org

Nashville Hiking Meetup Group
www.nashvillehiking.com

Hike Index

Other Tennessee Titles

Best Hikes Near Nashville

Insiders' Guide® to Nashville, 8th

Camping Tennessee

Hiking Tennessee

It Happened in Tennessee

Paddling Tennessee

Scenic Driving Tennessee

Tennessee Curiosities

Tennessee Off the Beaten Path®, 9th

About the Author

Keith Stelter is a columnist for the HCN newspaper group and has been hiking, writing, and taking photographs for forty years. He has hiked national park trails with his father and has hiked extensively in the Nashville area. His twin daughters were born in Nashville. Keith is a member of the Outdoor Writers Association of America, Texas Master Naturalists, North American Nature Photographers Association, and American Trails Association. He is the author of several books about Texas, including *Best Hikes near Austin and San Antonio, Best Hikes near Houston,* and *Best Easy Day Hikes* guides for Austin, Houston, and San Antonio. His avocation as a naturalist allows him to add interesting and educational information to his writing. Keith lives in Tomball, Texas.

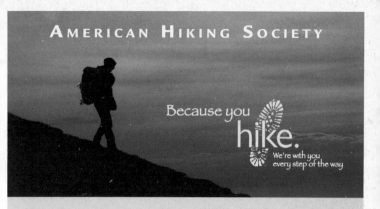

WHAT'S SO SPECIAL ABOUT UNSPOILED, NATURAL PLACES?

Beauty   Solitude   Wildness   Freedom   Quiet   Adventure
Serenity   Inspiration   Wonder   Excitement
Relaxation   Challenge

There's a lot to love about our treasured public lands, and the reasons are different for each of us. Whatever your reasons are, the national **Leave No Trace** education program will help you discover special outdoor places, enjoy them, and preserve them—today and for those who follow. By practicing and passing along these simple principles, you can help protect the special places you love from being loved to death.

THE PRINCIPLES OF **LEAVE NO TRACE**

- Plan ahead and prepare
- Travel and camp on durable surfaces
- Dispose of waste properly
- Leave what you find
- Minimize campfire impacts
- Respect wildlife
- Be considerate of other visitors